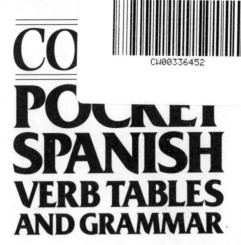

CO

POCKET
SPANISH
VERB TABLES
AND GRAMMAR

CW00336452

COLLINS
POCKET
SPANISH
VERB TABLES
AND GRAMMAR

HarperCollins*Publishers*

First published in this edition 1994

©HarperCollins Publishers 1994
First reprint 1996

ISBN 0 00 471013-4 Paperback

A de Benito de Harland
In consultation with
I F Ariza

editor
Jeremy Butterfield

editorial staff
Linda Chestnutt
Enrique González Sardinero

editorial management
Vivian Marr

*A catalogue record for this book
is available from the British Library*

All rights reserved

*Typeset by Morton Word Processing Ltd,
Scarborough*

*Printed in Great Britain by
HarperCollins Manufacturing, Glasgow*

This book has been designed to help all learners of Spanish to get to grips with the grammar of the language, whatever stage you are at in learning Spanish. For beginners, the book provides a clear introduction to all the basic rules and structures, and more advanced learners will find it an invaluable guide for reference and revision.

For ease of use, each part of speech (nouns, verbs, adjectives etc) has been treated separately (see the list of contents on the next page).

A special feature of this book is the clear demarcation of grammatical points, each treated on a left-hand page, and illustrated by examples in up-to-date Spanish on the opposite right-hand page. The appropriate example is clearly indicated by a system of bracketed numbers e.g. (→1), (→2) etc, corresponding to an example number on the facing page. Innovative use of colour highlights key learning points to provide maximum help for the user.

Special attention has been paid throughout to areas in which Spanish and English usage differ, thus helping the user to avoid the mistake of trying to translate English structures by identical structures in Spanish.

The tables of irregular verbs complement the extensive treatment of regular verbs in the grammar section of the book. In them 80 major irregular verbs are conjugated in their simple tenses so you can see where they differ from regular verbs. In addition, the verb index, in which all verbs are cross-referred to the appropriate conjugation model, enables you to check how over 2,800 Spanish verbs are conjugated.

A comprehensive index, containing key words in both Spanish and English, as well as subject references, completes the grammar.

Abbreviations used

algn	alguien	masc	masculine	pres	present
cond	conditional	p(p)	page(s)	sb	somebody
contd	continued	perf	perfect	sing	singular
fem	feminine	pluperf	pluperfect	sth	something
infin	infinitive	plur	plural	subj	subjunctive

4   CONTENTS

CONTENTS 5

Simple Tenses: Formation

In Spanish the simple tenses are:

Present	(→1)
Imperfect	(→2) – *past unfinished*
Future	(→3)
Conditional	(→4)
Preterite	(→5) – *past done*
Present Subjunctive	(→6)
Imperfect Subjunctive	(→7)

They are formed by adding endings to a verb stem. The endings show the number and person of the subject of the verb. (→8)

The stem and endings of regular verbs are totally predictable. The following sections show all the patterns for regular verbs. For irregular verbs see pp 80 ff.

Regular Verbs

There are three regular verb patterns (called conjugations), each identifiable by the ending of the infinitive:

• First conjugation verbs end in **-ar** e.g. **hablar** to speak

• Second conjugation verbs end in **-er** e.g. **comer** to eat

• Third conjugation verbs end in **-ir** e.g. **vivir** to live

These three conjugations are treated in order on the following pages. The subject pronouns will appear in brackets because they are not always necessary in Spanish (see p 226).

Continued

1 **(yo) habl**o
   I speak, I am speaking, I do speak

2 **(yo) habl**aba
   I spoke, I was speaking, I used to speak

3 **(yo) hablar**é
   I shall speak, I shall be speaking

4 **(yo) hablar**ía
   I should/would speak, I should/would be speaking

5 **(yo) habl**é
   I spoke

6 **(que) (yo) habl**e
   (that) I speak

7 **(que) (yo) habl**ara *or* **habl**ase
   (that) I speak

8 **(yo) habl**o I speak
   (nosotros) hablamos we speak
   (yo) hablaría I would speak
   (nosotros) hablaríamos we would speak

Simple Tenses: First Conjugation

● The stem is formed as follows:

TENSE	FORMATION	EXAMPLE
Present		
Imperfect		
Preterite	infinitive minus **-ar**	**habl-**
Present Subjunctive		
Imperfect Subjunctive		
Future	infinitive	**hablar-**
Conditional		

● To the appropriate stem add the following endings:

		PRESENT (→1)	IMPERFECT (→2)	PRETERITE (→3)
sing	1st person	**-o**	**-aba**	**-é**
	2nd person	**-as**	**-abas**	**-aste**
	3rd person	**-a**	**-aba**	**-ó**
plur	1st person	**-amos**	**-ábamos**	**-amos**
	2nd person	**-áis**	**-abais**	**-asteis**
	3rd person	**-an**	**-aban**	**-aron**

		PRESENT SUBJUNCTIVE (→4)	IMPERFECT SUBJUNCTIVE (→5)
sing	1st person	**-e**	**-ara** or **-ase**
	2nd person	**-es**	**-aras** or **-ases**
	3rd person	**-e**	**-ara** or **-ase**
plur	1st person	**-emos**	**-áramos** or **-ásemos**
	2nd person	**-éis**	**-arais** or **-aseis**
	3rd person	**-en**	**-aran** or **-asen**

		FUTURE (→6)	CONDITIONAL (→7)
sing	1st person	**-é**	**-ía**
	2nd person	**-ás**	**-ías**
	3rd person	**-á**	**-ía**
plur	1st person	**-emos**	**-íamos**
	2nd person	**-éis**	**-íais**
	3rd person	**-án**	**-ían**

1 *PRESENT*   **2** *IMPERFECT*   **3** *PRETERITE*

(yo)	hablo	hablaba	hablé
(tú)	hablas	hablabas	hablaste
(él/ella/Vd)	habla	hablaba	habló
(nosotros/as)	hablamos	hablábamos	hablamos
(vosotros/as)	habláis	hablabais	hablasteis
(ellos/as/Vds)	hablan	hablaban	hablaron

4 *PRESENT SUBJUNCTIVE*   **5** *IMPERFECT SUBJUNCTIVE*

(yo)	hable	hablara *or* hablase
(tú)	hables	hablaras *or* hablases
(él/ella/Vd)	hable	hablara *or* hablase
(nosotros/as)	hablemos	habláramos *or* hablásemos
(vosotros/as)	habléis	hablarais *or* hablaseis
(ellos/as/Vds)	hablen	hablaran *or* hablasen

6 *FUTURE*   **7** *CONDITIONAL*

(yo)	hablaré	hablaría
(tú)	hablarás	hablarías
(él/ella/Vd)	hablará	hablaría
(nosotros/as)	hablaremos	hablaríamos
(vosotros/as)	hablaréis	hablaríais
(ellos/as/Vds)	hablarán	hablarían

Simple Tenses: Second Conjugation

● The stem is formed as follows:

TENSE	FORMATION	EXAMPLE
Present		
Imperfect		
Preterite	infinitive minus **-er**	**com-**
Present Subjunctive		
Imperfect Subjunctive		
Future	infinitive	**comer-**
Conditional		

● To the appropriate stem add the following endings:

		PRESENT (→1)	IMPERFECT (→2)	PRETERITE (→3)
sing	1st person	**-o**	**-ía**	**-í**
	2nd person	**-es**	**-ías**	**-iste**
	3rd person	**-e**	**-ía**	**-ió**
plur	1st person	**-emos**	**-íamos**	**-imos**
	2nd person	**-éis**	**-íais**	**-isteis**
	3rd person	**-en**	**-ían**	**-ieron**

		PRESENT SUBJUNCTIVE (→4)	IMPERFECT SUBJUNCTIVE (→5)
sing	1st person	**-a**	**-iera** or **-iese**
	2nd person	**-as**	**-ieras** or **-ieses**
	3rd person	**-a**	**-iera** or **-iese**
plur	1st person	**-amos**	**-iéramos** or **-iésemos**
	2nd person	**-áis**	**-ierais** or **-ieseis**
	3rd person	**-an**	**-ieran** or **-iesen**

		FUTURE (→6)	CONDITIONAL (→7)
sing	1st person	**-é**	**-ía**
	2nd person	**-ás**	**-ías**
	3rd person	**-á**	**-ía**
plur	1st person	**-emos**	**-íamos**
	2nd person	**-éis**	**-íais**
	3rd person	**-án**	**-ían**

1 *PRESENT*

(yo)	como
(tú)	comes
(él/ella/Vd)	come
(nosotros/as)	comemos
(vosotros/as)	coméis
(ellos/as/Vds)	comen

2 *IMPERFECT*

comía
comías
comía
comíamos
comíais
comían

3 *PRETERITE*

comí
comiste
comió
comimos
comisteis
comieron

4 *PRESENT SUBJUNCTIVE*

(yo)	coma
(tú)	comas
(él/ella/Vd)	coma
(nosotros/as)	comamos
(vosotros/as)	comáis
(ellos/as/Vds)	coman

5 *IMPERFECT SUBJUNCTIVE*

comiera *or* comiese
comieras *or* comieses
comiera *or* comiese
comiéramos *or* comiésemos
comierais *or* comieseis
comieran *or* comiesen

6 *FUTURE*

(yo)	comeré
(tú)	comerás
(él/ella/Vd)	comerá
(nosotros/as)	comeremos
(vosotros/as)	comeréis
(ellos/as/Vds)	comerán

7 *CONDITIONAL*

comería
comerías
comería
comeríamos
comeríais
comerían

Simple Tenses: Third Conjugation

● The stem is formed as follows:

TENSE	FORMATION	EXAMPLE
Present		
Imperfect		
Preterite	infinitive minus -ir	viv-
Present Subjunctive		
Imperfect Subjunctive		
Future	infinitive	vivir-
Conditional		

● To the appropriate stem add the following endings:

		PRESENT (→1)	IMPERFECT (→2)	PRETERITE (→3)
sing	1st person	-o	-ía	-í
	2nd person	-es	-ías	-iste
	3rd person	-e	-ía	-ió
plur	1st person	-imos	-íamos	-imos
	2nd person	-ís	-íais	-isteis
	3rd person	-en	-ían	-ieron

		PRESENT SUBJUNCTIVE (→4)	IMPERFECT SUBJUNCTIVE (→5)
sing	1st person	-a	-iera or -iese
	2nd person	-as	-ieras or -ieses
	3rd person	-a	-iera or -iese
plur	1st person	-amos	-iéramos or -iésemos
	2nd person	-áis	-ierais or -ieseis
	3rd person	-an	-ieran or -iesen

		FUTURE (→6)	CONDITIONAL (→7)
sing	1st person	-é	-ía
	2nd person	-ás	-ías
	3rd person	-á	-ía
plur	1st person	-emos	-íamos
	2nd person	-éis	-íais
	3rd person	-án	-ían

Examples

[handwritten: wrong / incomplete] VE

1 *PRESENT*

		2 *IMPERFECT*	**3** *PRE*
(yo)	vivo	vivía	viví
(tú)	vives	vivías	viviste
(él/ella/Vd)	vive	vivía	vivió
(nosotros/as)	vivimos	vivíamos	vivimos
(vosotros/as)	vivís	vivíais	vivisteis
(ellos/as/Vds)	viven	vivían	vivieron

4 *PRESENT SUBJUNCTIVE*   **5** *IMPERFECT SUBJUNCTIVE*

(yo)	viva	viviera *or* viviese
(tú)	vivas	vivieras *or* vivieses
(él/ella/Vd)	viva	viviera *or* viviese
(nosotros/as)	vivamos	viviéramos *or* viviésemos
(vosotros/as)	viváis	vivierais *or* vivieseis
(ellos/as/Vds)	vivan	vivieran *or* viviesen

6 *FUTURE*   **7** *CONDITIONAL*

(yo)	viviré	viviría
(tú)	vivirás	vivirías
(él/ella/Vd)	vivirá	viviría
(nosotros/as)	viviremos	viviríamos
(vosotros/as)	viviréis	viviríais
(ellos/as/Vds)	vivirán	vivirían

... verb used to give commands or
... ely, as in English 'Shut the door,

... s, the imperative forms for **Vd, Vds** and
... e as the subjunctive. The other forms are as

... 3rd person singular present indicative)
... (final **-r** of infinitive changes to **-d**) (→1)

	habla *speak*	**come** *eat*	**vive** *live*
	hable *speak*	**coma** *eat*	**viva** *live*
(nosotros)	**hablemos** *let's speak*	**comamos** *let's eat*	**vivamos** *let's live*
(vosotros)	**hablad** *speak*	**comed** *eat*	**vivid** *live*
(Vds)	**hablen** *speak*	**coman** *eat*	**vivan** *live*

In NEGATIVE commands, all the imperative forms are exactly the same as the present subjunctive.

• The imperative of irregular verbs is given in the verb tables, pp 82 ff.

Position of object pronouns with the imperative

In POSITIVE commands: they follow the verb and are attached to it. An accent is needed to show the correct position for stress (see p 292) (→2)

In NEGATIVE commands: they precede the verb and are not attached to it (→3)

• For the order of object pronouns, see page 232.

Continued

1 **cantar**
to sing

cantad
sing

2 **Perdóneme**
Excuse me
Elíjanos
Choose us
Esperémosla
Let's wait for her/it

Enviémoselos
Let's send them to him/her/them
Explíquemelo
Explain it to me
Devuélvaselo
Give it back to him/her/them

3 **No me molestes**
Don't disturb me

No les castiguemos
Let's not punish them
No las conteste
Don't answer them

No se la devolvamos
Let's not give it back to him/her/them
No me lo mandes
Don't send it to me
No nos lo hagan
Don't do it to us

16 VERBS

The Imperative (contd)

- For reflexive verbs – e.g. **levantarse** *to get up* – the object pronoun is the reflexive pronoun. It should be noted that the imperative forms need an accent to show the correct position for stress (see p 292). The forms **nosotros** and **vosotros** also drop the final **-s** and **-d** respectively before the pronoun (→**1**)

  EXCEPTION: **idos (vosotros)** *go*

- Note: For general instructions, the infinitive is used instead of the imperative (→**2**), but when it is preceded by **vamos a** it often translates *let's* ... (→**3**)

1 Levántate   No te levantes
   Get up   Don't get up
   Levántese (Vd)   **No se levante (Vd)**
   Get up   Don't get up
   Levantémonos   **No nos levantemos**
   Let's get up   Let's not get up
   Levantaos   **No os levantéis**
   Get up   Don't get up
   Levántense (Vds) **No se levanten (Vds)**
   Get up   Don't get up

2 Ver pág ...
   See page ...
   No pasar
   Do not pass

3 Vamos a ver
   Let's see
   Vamos a empezar
   Let's start

Compound Tenses: Formation

In Spanish the compound tenses are:

Perfect	(→1)
Pluperfect	(→2)
Future Perfect	(→3)
Conditional Perfect	(→4)
Past Anterior	(→5)
Perfect Subjunctive	(→6)
Pluperfect Subjunctive	(→7)

They consist of the past participle of the verb together with the auxiliary verb **haber**.

Compound tenses are formed in exactly the same way for both regular and irregular verbs, the only difference being that irregular verbs may have an irregular past participle.

The Past Participle

For all compound tenses you need to know how to form the past participle of the verb. For regular verbs this is as follows:

- 1st conjugation: replace the **-ar** of the infinitive by **-ado** (→8)

- 2nd conjugation: replace the **-er** of the infinitive by **-ido** (→9)

- 3rd conjugation: replace the **-ir** of the infinitive by **-ido** (→10)

Continued

1 **(yo) he habl**ado
  I speak, I have spoken

2 **(yo)** había **habl**ado
  I had spoken

3 **(yo)** habré **habl**ado
  I shall have spoken

4 **(yo)** habría **habl**ado
  I should/would have spoken

5 **(yo)** hube **habl**ado
  I had spoken

6 **(que) (yo)** haya **habl**ado
  (that) I spoke, have spoken

7 **(que) (yo)** hubiera/hubiese **habl**ado
  (that) I had spoken

8 **cant**ar → **cant**ado
  to speak   spoken

9 **com**er → **com**ido
  to eat   eaten

10 **viv**ir → **viv**ido
   to live   lived

Compound Tenses: formation (contd)

Perfect tense:

the present tense of **haber** plus the past participle (→**1**)

Pluperfect tense:

the imperfect tense of **haber** plus the past participle (→**2**)

Future Perfect:

the future tense of **haber** plus the past participle (→**3**)

Conditional Perfect:

the conditional of **haber** plus the past participle (→**4**)

Continued

1 *PERFECT*

(yo)	**he** hablado
(tú)	**has** hablado
(él/ella/Vd)	**ha** hablado
(nosotros/as)	**hemos** hablado
(vosotros/as)	**habéis** hablado
(ellos/as/Vds)	**han** hablado

2 *PLUPERFECT*

(yo)	**había** hablado
(tú)	**habías** hablado
(él/ella/Vd)	**había** hablado
(nosotros/as)	**habíamos** hablado
(vosotros/as)	**habíais** hablado
(ellos/as/Vds)	**habían** hablado

3 *FUTURE PERFECT*

(yo)	**habré** hablado
(tú)	**habrás** hablado
(él/ella/Vd)	**habrá** hablado
(nosotros/as)	**habremos** hablado
(vosotros/as)	**habréis** hablado
(ellos/as/Vds)	**habrán** hablado

4 *CONDITIONAL PERFECT*

(yo)	**habría** hablado
(tú)	**habrías** hablado
(él/ella/Vd)	**habría** hablado
(nosotros/as)	**habríamos** hablado
(vosotros/as)	**habríais** hablado
(ellos/as/Vds)	**habrían** hablado

Compound Tenses: formation (contd)

Past Anterior: the preterite of **haber** plus the past
                              participle (→1)

Perfect Subjunctive: the present subjunctive of **haber** plus the
                              past participle (→2)

Pluperfect Subjunctive: the imperfect subjunctive of **haber** plus
                              the past participle (→3)

- For how to form the past participle of regular verbs see p 18.
  The past participle of irregular verbs is given for each verb in
  the verb tables, pp 82 to 161.

1 *PAST ANTERIOR*

(yo)	hube hablado
(tú)	hubiste hablado
(él/ella/Vd)	hubo hablado
(nosotros/as)	hubimos hablado
(vosotros/as)	hubisteis hablado
(ellos/as/Vds)	hubieron hablado

2 *PRESENT SUBJUNCTIVE*

(yo)	haya hablado
(tú)	hayas hablado
(él/ella/Vd)	haya hablado
(nosotros/as)	hayamos hablado
(vosotros/as)	hayáis hablado
(ellos/as/Vds)	hayan hablado

3 *PLUPERFECT SUBJUNCTIVE*

(yo)	hubiera *or* hubiese hablado
(tú)	hubieras *or* hubieses hablado
(él/ella/Vd)	hubiera *or* hubiese hablado
(nosotros/as)	hubiéramos *or* hubiésemos hablado
(vosotros/as)	hubierais *or* hubieseis hablado
(ellos/as/Vds)	hubieran *or* hubiesen hablado

Reflexive Verbs

A reflexive verb is one accompanied by a reflexive pronoun. The infinitive of a reflexive verb ends with the pronoun **se**, which is added to the verb form e.g.
levantarse *to get up*; **lavarse** *to wash (oneself)*.

The reflexive pronouns are:

PERSON	SINGULAR	PLURAL
1st	**me**	**nos**
2nd	**te**	**os**
3rd	**se**	**se**

- The reflexive pronoun 'reflects back' to the subject, but it is not always translated in English (→**1**)
  The plural pronouns are sometimes translated as *one another, each other* (the 'reciprocal' meaning) (→**2**)
  The reciprocal meaning may be emphasized by **el uno al otro/la una a la otra (los unos a los otros/las unas a las otras)** (→**3**)

- Both simple and compound tenses of reflexive verbs are conjugated in exactly the same way as those of non-reflexive verbs, except that the reflexive pronoun is always used.
  The only irregularity is in the 1st and 2nd person plural of the affirmative imperative (see p 16). A sample reflexive verb is conjugated in full on pp 28 to 31.

Position of reflexive pronouns

- Except with the infinitive, gerund and positive commands the pronoun comes before the verb (→**4**)

- In the infinitive, gerund and positive commands, the pronoun follows the verb and is attached to it (but see also p 228) (→**5**)

Continued

1 **Me visto**
  I'm dressing (myself)
  Nos lavamos
  We're washing (ourselves)
  Se levanta
  He gets up

2 **Nos queremos**
  We love each other
  Se parecen
  They resemble one another

3 **Se miraban** el uno al otro
  They were looking at each other

4 **Me acuesto temprano**
  I go to bed early
  ¿Cómo se llama Vd?
  What is your name?
  No se ha despertado
  He hasn't woken up
  No te levantes
  Don't get up

5 **Quiero irme**
  I want to go away
  Estoy levantándome
  I am getting up
  Siéntense
  Sit down
  Vámonos
  Let's go

Reflexive Verbs (contd)

Some verbs have both a reflexive and non-reflexive form. When used reflexively, they have a different but closely related meaning, as shown in the following examples.

NON-REFLEXIVE	*REFLEXIVE*
acostar *to put to bed*	**acostarse** *to go to bed*
casar *to marry (off)*	**casarse** *to get married*
detener *to stop*	**detenerse** *to come to a halt*
dormir *to sleep*	**dormirse** *to go to sleep*
enfadar *to annoy*	**enfadarse** *to get annoyed*
hacer *to make*	**hacerse** *to become*
ir *to go*	**irse** *to leave, go away*
lavar *to wash*	**lavarse** *to get washed*
levantar *to raise*	**levantarse** *to get up*
llamar *to call*	**llamarse** *to be called*
poner *to put*	**ponerse** *to put on (clothing), to become*
sentir *to feel (something)*	**sentirse** *to feel (sick, tired, etc)*
vestir *to dress (someone)*	**vestirse** *to get dressed*
volver *to return*	**volverse** *to turn round*

- Some other verbs exist only in the reflexive:

arrepentirse *to repent*	**jactarse** *to boast*
atreverse *to dare*	**quejarse** *to complain*

- Some verbs acquire a different nuance when used reflexively:

caer *to fall* (→1)	**caerse** *to fall down (by accident)* (→2)
morir *to die, be killed (by accident or on purpose)* (→3)	**morirse** *to die (from natural causes)* (→4)

- Often a reflexive verb can be used:
  - to avoid the passive (see p 34) (→5)
  - in impersonal expressions (see p 40) (→6)

Continued

1 **El agua** caía **desde las rocas**
   Water fell from the rocks

2 **Me caí y me rompí el brazo**
   I fell and broke my arm

3 **Tres personas** han muerto **en un accidente/atentado terro-
   rista**
   Three people were killed in an accident/a terrorist attack

4 **Mi abuelo** se murió **a los ochenta años**
   My grandfather died at the age of eighty

5 Se perdió **la batalla**
   The battle was lost
   No se veían **las casas**
   The houses could not be seen

6 Se dice **que** ...
   (It is said that) People say that ...
   No se puede **entrar**
   You/One can't go in
   No se permite
   It is not allowed

Reflexive Verbs (contd)

Conjugation of: **lavarse** *to wash oneself*

I *SIMPLE TENSES*

PRESENT

(yo)	**me lavo**
(tú)	**te lavas**
(él/ella/Vd)	**se lava**
(nosotros/as)	**nos lavamos**
(vosotros/as)	**os laváis**
(ellos/as/Vds)	**se lavan**

IMPERFECT

(yo)	**me lavaba**
(tú)	**te lavabas**
(él/ella/Vd)	**se lavaba**
(nosotros/as)	**nos lavábamos**
(vosotros/as)	**os lavabais**
(ellos/as/Vds)	**se lavaban**

FUTURE

(yo)	**me lavaré**
(tú)	**te lavarás**
(él/ella/Vd)	**se lavará**
(nosotros/as)	**nos lavaremos**
(vosotros/as)	**os lavaréis**
(ellos/as/Vds)	**se lavarán**

CONDITIONAL

(yo)	**me lavaría**
(tú)	**te lavarías**
(él/ella/Vd)	**se lavaría**
(nosotros/as)	**nos lavaríamos**
(vosotros/as)	**os lavaríais**
(ellos/as/Vds)	**se lavarían**

Reflexive Verbs (contd)

Conjugation of: **lavarse** to wash oneself

I *SIMPLE TENSES*

PRETERITE

(yo)	**me** lavé
(tú)	**te** lavaste
(él/ella/Vd)	**se** lavó
(nosotros/as)	**nos** lavamos
(vosotros/as)	**os** lavasteis
(ellos/as/Vds)	**se** lavaron

PRESENT SUBJUNCTIVE

(yo)	**me** lave
(tú)	**te** laves
(él/ella/Vd)	**se** lave
(nosotros/as)	**nos** lavemos
(vosotros/as)	**os** lavéis
(ellos/as/Vds)	**se** laven

IMPERFECT SUBJUNCTIVE

(yo)	**me** lavara *or* lavase
(tú)	**te** lavaras *or* lavases
(él/ella/Vd)	**se** lavara *or* lavase
(nosotros/as)	**nos** laváramos *or* lavásemos
(vosotros/as)	**os** lavarais *or* lavaseis
(ellos/as/Vds)	**se** lavaran *or* lavasen

Continued

Reflexive Verbs (contd)

Conjugation of: **lavarse** *to wash oneself*

II *COMPOUND TENSES*

PERFECT

(yo)	me he lavado
(tú)	te has lavado
(él/ella/Vd)	se ha lavado
(nosotros/as)	nos hemos lavado
(vosotros/as)	os habéis lavado
(ellos/as/Vds)	se han lavado

PLUPERFECT

(yo)	me había lavado
(tú)	te habías lavado
(él/ella/Vd)	se había lavado
(nosotros/as)	nos habíamos lavado
(vosotros/as)	os habíais lavado
(ellos/as/Vds)	se habían lavado

FUTURE PERFECT

(yo)	me habré lavado
(tú)	te habrás lavado
(él/ella/Vd)	se habrá lavado
(nosotros/as)	nos habremos lavado
(vosotros/as)	os habréis lavado
(ellos/as/Vds)	se habrán lavado

Reflexive Verbs (contd)

Conjugation of: **lavarse** *to wash oneself*

II *COMPOUND TENSES*

PAST ANTERIOR

(yo)	**me hube** lavado
(tú)	**te hubiste** lavado
(él/ella/Vd)	**se hubo** lavado
(nosotros/as)	**nos hubimos** lavado
(vosotros/as)	**os hubisteis** lavado
(ellos/as/Vds)	**se hubieron** lavado

PERFECT SUBJUNCTIVE

(yo)	**me haya** lavado
(tú)	**te hayas** lavado
(él/ella/Vd)	**se haya** lavado
(nosotros/as)	**nos hayamos** lavado
(vosotros/as)	**os hayáis** lavado
(ellos/as/Vds)	**se hayan** lavado

PLUPERFECT SUBJUNCTIVE

(yo)	**me hubiera** *or* **hubiese** lavado
(tú)	**te hubieras** *or* **hubieses** lavado
(él/ella/Vd)	**se hubiera** *or* **hubiese** lavado
(nosotros/as)	**nos hubiéramos** *or* **hubiésemos** lavado
(vosotros/as)	**os hubierais** *or* **hubieseis** lavado
(ellos/as/Vds)	**se hubieran** *or* **hubiesen** lavado

The Passive

In active sentences, the subject of a verb carries out the action of that verb, but in passive sentences the subject receives the action. Compare the following:
  The car hit Jane (subject: *the car*)
  Jane was hit by the car (subject: *Jane*)

- English uses the verb '*to be*' with the past participle to form passive sentences. Spanish forms them in the same way, i.e.:
    a tense of **ser** + past participle
  The past participle agrees in number and gender with the subject (→**1**)

A sample verb is conjugated in the passive voice on pp 36 to 39.

- In English, the word '*by*' usually introduces the agent through which the action of a passive sentence is performed. In Spanish this agent is preceded by **por** (→**2**)

- The Passive voice is used much less frequently in Spanish than English. It is, however, often used in expressions where the identity of the agent is unknown or unimportant (→**3**)

Continued

1 **Pablo** ha sido despedido
  Paul has been sacked
  Su madre era **muy** admirada
  His mother was greatly admired
  El palacio será vendido
  The palace will be sold
  Las puertas habían sido cerradas
  The doors had been closed

2 **La casa** fue diseñada por **mi hermano**
  The house was designed by my brother

3 **La ciudad** fue conquistada **tras un largo asedio**
  The city was conquered after a long siege
  Ha sido declarado el estado de excepción
  A state of emergency has been declared

The Passive (contd)

In English the indirect object in an active sentence can become the subject of the related passive sentence,
e.g. *His mother gave him the book* (indirect object: *him*)
     He was given the book by his mother

This is not possible in Spanish. The indirect object remains as such, while the object of the active sentence becomes the subject of the passive sentence (→1)

Other ways to express a passive meaning

Since modern Spanish tends to avoid the passive, it uses various other constructions to replace it:

- If the agent (person or object performing the action) is known, the active is often preferred where English might prefer the passive (→2)

- The 3rd person plural of the active voice can be used. The meaning is equivalent to *they* + verb (→3)

- When the action of the sentence is performed on a person, the reflexive form of the verb can be used in the 3rd person singular, and the person becomes the object (→4)

- When the action is performed on a thing, this becomes the subject of the sentence and the verb is made reflexive, agreeing in number with the subject (→5)

Continued

1 **Su madre** le regaló **el libro**
His mother gave him the book
becomes
El libro le fue regalado **por su madre**
The book was given to him by his mother

2 **La policía** interrogó **al sospechoso**
The police questioned the suspect
rather than
El sospechoso fue interrogado **por la policía**

3 **Usan demasiada publicidad en la televisión**
Too much advertising is used on television

4 **Últimamente no** se le/les ha visto **mucho en público**
He has/they have not been seen much in public recently

5 **Esta palabra ya no** se usa
This word is no longer used
Todos los libros se han vendido
All the books have been sold

The Passive (contd)

Conjugation of: **ser amado** *to be loved*

PRESENT

(yo)	**soy** amado(a)
(tú)	**eres** amado(a)
(él/ella/Vd)	**es** amado(a)
(nosotros/as)	**somos** amado(a)s
(vosotros/as)	**sois** amado(a)s
(ellos/as/Vds)	**son** amado(a)s

IMPERFECT

(yo)	**era** amado(a)
(tú)	**eras** amado(a)
(él/ella/Vd)	**era** amado(a)
(nosotros/as)	**éramos** amado(a)s
(vosotros/as)	**erais** amado(a)s
(ellos/as/Vds)	**eran** amado(a)s

FUTURE

(yo)	**seré** amado(a)
(tú)	**serás** amado(a)
(él/ella/Vd)	**será** amado(a)
(nosotros/as)	**seremos** amado(a)s
(vosotros/as)	**seréis** amado(a)s
(ellos/as/Vds)	**serán** amado(a)s

CONDITIONAL

(yo)	**sería** amado(a)
(tú)	**serías** amado(a)
(él/ella/Vd)	**sería** amado(a)
(nosotros/as)	**seríamos** amado(a)s
(vosotros/as)	**seríais** amado(a)s
(ellos/as/Vds)	**serían** amado(a)s

The Passive (contd)

Conjugation of: **ser amado** *to be loved*

PRETERITE

(yo)	**fui** amado(a)
(tú)	**fuiste** amado(a)
(él/ella/Vd)	**fue** amado(a)
(nosotros/as)	**fuimos** amado(a)s
(vosotros/as)	**fuisteis** amado(a)s
(ellos/as/Vds)	**fueron** amado(a)s

PRESENT SUBJUNCTIVE

(yo)	**sea** amado(a)
(tú)	**seas** amado(a)
(él/ella/Vd)	**sea** amado(a)
(nosotros/as)	**seamos** amado(a)s
(vosotros/as)	**seáis** amado(a)s
(ellos/as/Vds)	**sean** amado(a)s

IMPERFECT SUBJUNCTIVE

(yo)	**fuera** *or* **fuese** amado(a)
(tú)	**fueras** *or* **fueses** amado(a)
(él/ella/Vd)	**fuera** *or* **fuese** amado(a)
(nosotros/as)	**fuéramos** *or* **fuésemos** amado(a)s
(vosotros/as)	**fuerais** *or* **fueseis** amado(a)s
(ellos/as/Vds)	**fueran** *or* **fuesen** amado(a)s

Continued

The Passive (contd)

Conjugation of: **ser amado** *to be loved*

PERFECT

(yo)	he sido amado(a)
(tú)	has sido amado(a)
(él/ella/Vd)	ha sido amado(a)
(nosotros/as)	hemos sido amado(a)s
(vosotros/as)	habéis sido amado(a)s
(ellos/as/Vds)	han sido amado(a)s

PLUPERFECT

(yo)	había sido amado(a)
(tú)	habías sido amado(a)
(él/ella/Vd)	había sido amado(a)
(nosotros/as)	habíamos sido amado(a)s
(vosotros/as)	habíais sido amado(a)s
(ellos/as/Vds)	habían sido amado(a)s

FUTURE PERFECT

(yo)	habré sido amado(a)
(tú)	habrás sido amado(a)
(él/ella/Vd)	habrá sido amado(a)
(nosotros/as)	habremos sido amado(a)s
(vosotros/as)	habréis sido amado(a)s
(ellos/as/Vds)	habrán sido amado(a)s

CONDITIONAL PERFECT

(yo)	habría sido amado(a)
(tú)	habrías sido amado(a)
(él/ella/Vd)	habría sido amado(a)
(nosotros/as)	habríamos sido amado(a)s
(vosotros/as)	habríais sido amado(a)s
(ellos/as/Vds)	habrían sido amado(a)s

The Passive (contd)

Conjugation of: **ser amado** *to be loved*

PAST ANTERIOR

(yo)	**hube sido amado(a)**
(tú)	**hubiste sido amado(a)**
(él/ella/Vd)	**hubo sido amado(a)**
(nosotros/as)	**hubimos sido amado(a)s**
(vosotros/as)	**hubisteis sido amado(a)s**
(ellos/as/Vds)	**hubieron sido amado(a)s**

PERFECT SUBJUNCTIVE

(yo)	**haya sido amado(a)**
(tú)	**hayas sido amado(a)**
(él/ella/Vd)	**haya sido amado(a)**
(nosotros/as)	**hayamos sido amado(a)s**
(vosotros/as)	**hayáis sido amado(a)s**
(ellos/as/Vds)	**hayan sido amado(a)s**

PLUPERFECT SUBJUNCTIVE

(yo)	**hubiera/-se sido amado(a)**
(tú)	**hubieras/-ses sido amado(a)**
(él/ella/Vd)	**hubiera/-se sido amado(a)**
(nosotros/as)	**hubiéramos/-semos sido amado(a)s**
(vosotros/as)	**hubierais/-seis sido amado(a)s**
(ellos/as/Vds)	**hubieran/-sen sido amado(a)s**

Impersonal Verbs

Impersonal verbs are used only in the infinitive, the gerund, and in the 3rd person (usually singular); unlike English, Spanish does not use the subject pronoun with impersonal verbs.

e.g. **llueve**
  it's raining
  es fácil decir que ...
  it's easy to say that ...

The most common impersonal verbs are:

INFINITIVE	CONSTRUCTION	
amanecer	**amanece/está amaneciendo**	
	it's daybreak	
anochecer	**anochece/está anocheciendo**	
	it's getting dark	
granizar	**graniza/está granizando**	
	it's hailing	
llover	**llueve/está lloviendo**	(→1)
	it's raining	
lloviznar	**llovizna/está lloviznando**	
	it's drizzling	
nevar	**nieva/está nevando**	
	it's snowing	
tronar	**truena/está tronando**	
	it's thundering	

Some reflexive verbs are also used impersonally.
The most common are:

INFINITIVE	CONSTRUCTION
creerse	**se cree que*** + indicative (→2)
	it is thought that; people think that
decirse	**se dice que*** + indicative (→3)
	it is said that; people say that

Continued

1 Llovía a cántaros
It was raining cats and dogs
Estaba nevando cuando salieron
It was snowing when they left

2 Se cree que llegarán mañana
It is thought they will arrive tomorrow

3 Se dice que ha sido el peor invierno en 50 años
People say it's been the worst winter in 50 years

Impersonal Verbs (contd)

INFINITIVE	CONSTRUCTION
poderse	**se puede** + infinitive (→1)
	one/people can, it is possible to
tratarse de	**se trata de** + noun (→2)
	it's a question/matter of something
	it's about something
	se trata de + infinitive (→3)
	it's a question/matter of doing; somebody must do
venderse	**se vende*** + noun (→4)
	to be sold; for sale

*This impersonal construction conveys the same meaning as the 3rd person plural of these verbs; **creen que, dicen que, venden**

The following verbs are also commonly used in impersonal contructions:

INFINITIVE	CONSTRUCTION
bastar	**basta con** + infinitive (→5)
	it is enough to do
	basta con + noun (→6)
	something is enough, it only takes sth
faltar	**falta** + infinitive (→7)
	we still have to/one still has to
haber	**hay** + noun (→8)
	there is/are
	hay que + infinitive (→9)
	one has to/we have to
hacer	**hace** + noun/adjective depicting weather/dark/ light etc (→10)
	it is
	hace + time expression + **que** + indicative (→11)
	somebody has done or been doing something since ...
	hace + time expression + **que** + negative indicative (→12)
	it is ... since

Continued

1 **Aquí se puede aparcar**
One can park here

2 **No se trata de dinero**
It isn't a question/matter of money

3 **Se trata de poner fin al asunto**
We must put an end to the matter

4 **Se vende coche**
Car for sale

5 **Basta con telefonear para reservar un asiento**
You need only phone to reserve a seat

6 **Basta con un error para que todo se estropee**
One single error is enough to ruin everything

7 **Aún falta cerrar las maletas**
We/One still have/has to close the suitcases

8 **Hay una habitación libre**
There is one spare room
No había cartas esta mañana
There were no letters this morning

9 **Hay que cerrar las puertas**
We have/One has to shut the doors

10 **Hace calor/viento/sol**
It is hot/windy/sunny
Mañana hará bueno
It'll be nice (weather) tomorrow

11 **Hace seis meses que vivo/vivimos aquí**
I/we have lived *or* been living here for six months

12 **Hace tres años que no le veo**
It is three years since I last saw him

Impersonal Verbs (contd)

INFINITIVE	*CONSTRUCTION*
hacer falta	**hace falta** + noun object (+ indirect object) (→1) *(somebody) needs something, something is necessary (to somebody)* **hace falta** + infinitive (+ indirect object) (→2) *it is necessary to do* **hace falta que** + subjunctive (→3) *it is necessary to do, somebody must do*
parecer	**parece que** (+ indirect object) + indicative (→4) *it seems/appears that*
ser	**es/son** + time expression (→5) *it is* **es** + **de día/noche** (→6) *it is* **es** + adjective + infinitive (→7) *it is*
ser mejor	**es mejor** + infinitive (→8) *it's better to do* **es mejor que** + subjunctive (→9) *it's better if/that*
valer más	**más vale** + infinitive (→10) *it's better to do* **más vale que** + subjunctive (→11) *it's better to do/that somebody does*

1   **Hace falta valor para hacer eso**
    One needs courage to do that; Courage is needed to do that
    Me hace falta otro vaso más
    I need an extra glass
2   **Hace falta volver**
    It is necessary to return; We/I/You must return*
    Me hacía falta volver
    I had to return
3   **Hace falta que Vd se vaya**
    You have to/must leave
4   **(Me) parece que estás equivocado**
    It seems (to me) you are wrong
5   **Son las tres y media**
    It is half past three
    Ya es primavera
    It is Spring now
6   **Era de noche cuando llegamos**
    It was night when we arrived
7   **Era inútil protestar**
    It was useless to complain
8   **Es mejor no decir nada**
    It's better to keep quiet
9   **Es mejor que lo pongas aquí**
    It's better if/that you put it here
10 **Más vale prevenir que curar**
    Prevention is better than cure
11 **Más valdría que no fuéramos**
    It would be better if we didn't go/We'd better not go

*The translation here obviously depends on context

The Infinitive

The infinitive is the form of the verb found in dictionary entries meaning '*to ...*', e.g. **hablar** *to speak*, **vivir** *to live*.

The infinitive is used in the following ways:
- After a preposition (→1)

- As a verbal noun (→2)
  In this use the article may precede the infinitive, especially when the infinitive is the subject and begins the sentence (→3)

- As a dependent infinitive, in the following verbal constructions:
  - —with no linking preposition (→4)
  - —with the linking preposition **a** (→5)
    (see also p 66)
  - —with the linking preposition **de** (→6)
    (see also p 66)
  - —with the linking preposition **en** (→7)
    (see also p 66)
  - —with the linking preposition **con** (→8)
    (see also p 66)
  - —with the linking preposition **por** (→9)
    (see also p 66)

- The following construction should also be noted:
  indefinite pronoun + **que** + infinitive (→10)

- The object pronouns generally follow the infinitive and are attached to it. For exceptions see p 228.

Continued

Examples

1 Después de acabar **el desayuno, salió de casa**
  After finishing her breakfast she went out
  Al enterarse de lo ocurrido se puso furiosa
  When she found out what had happened she was furious
  Me hizo daño sin saberlo
  She hurt me without her knowing

2 **Su deporte preferido es** montar a caballo
  Her favourite sport is horse riding
  Ver es creer
  Seeing is believing

3 El viajar **tanto me resulta cansado**
  I find so much travelling tiring

4 **¿Quiere Vd** esperar?
  Would you like to wait?

5 **Aprenderán pronto** a nadar
  They will soon learn to swim

6 **Pronto dejará** de llover
  It'll stop raining soon

7 **La comida tarda** en hacerse
  The meal is taking a long time to cook

8 **Amenazó** con denunciarles
  He threatened to report them (to the police)

9 **Comience Vd** por decirme su nombre
  Please start by giving me your name

10 **Tengo** algo que decirte
  I have something to tell you

The Infinitive (contd)

The verbs set out below are followed by the infinitive with no linking preposition.

- **deber, poder, saber, querer** and **tener que** (**hay que** in impersonal constructions) (→**1**)

- **valer más, hacer falta**: see Impersonal Verbs, p 44

- verbs of seeing or hearing e.g. **ver** to see, **oír** to hear (→**2**)

- **hacer** (→**3**)

- **dejar** to let, allow (→**3**)

- The following common verbs:

aconsejar	to advise	(→**4**)
conseguir	to manage to	(→**5**)
decidir	to decide	
desear	to wish, want	(→**6**)
esperar	to hope	(→**7**)
evitar	to avoid	(→**8**)
impedir	to prevent	(→**9**)
intentar	to try	(→**10**)
lograr	to manage to	(→**5**)
necesitar	to need	(→**11**)
odiar	to hate	
olvidar	to forget	(→**12**)
pensar	to think	(→**13**)
preferir	to prefer	(→**14**)
procurar	to try	(→**10**)
prohibir	to forbid	(→**15**)
prometer	to promise	(→**16**)
proponer	to propose	(→**17**)

Continued

1 **¿Quiere Vd esperar?**
Would you like to wait?
No puede venir
She can't come

2 **Nos** ha visto llegar   **Se les** oye cantar
She saw us arriving   You can hear them singing

3 **No me** hagas reír   **Déjeme** pasar
Don't make me laugh   Let me past

4 **Le** aconsejamos dejar**lo para mañana**
We advise you to leave it until tomorrow

5 **Aún no he** conseguido/logrado **entenderlo**
I still haven't managed to understand it

6 **No** desea tener **más hijos**
She doesn't want to have any more children

7 **Esperamos ir** de vacaciones este verano
We are hoping to go on holiday this summer

8 **Evite beber cuando conduzca**
Avoid drinking and driving

9 **No pudo** impedir**le hablar**
He couldn't prevent him from speaking

10 **Intentamos/procuramos pasar desapercibidos**
We tried not to be noticed

11 **Necesitaba salir a la calle**
I/he/she needed to go out

12 **Olvidó dejar su dirección**
He/she forgot to leave his/her address

13 **¿Piensan venir por Navidad?**
Are you thinking of coming for Christmas?

14 **Preferiría elegirlo yo mismo**
I'd rather choose it myself

15 **Prohibió fumar a los alumnos**
He forbade the pupils to smoke

16 **Prometieron volver pronto**
They promised to come back soon

17 **Propongo salir cuanto antes**
I propose to leave as soon as possible

The Infinitive: Set Expressions

The following are set in Spanish with the meaning shown:

dejar caer	*to drop*	(→**1**)
hacer entrar	*to show in*	(→**2**)
hacer saber	*to let know, make known*	(→**3**)
hacer salir	*to let out*	(→**4**)
hacer venir	*to send for*	(→**5**)
ir(se) a buscar	*to go for, go and get*	(→**6**)
mandar hacer	*to order*	(→**7**)
mandar llamar	*to send for*	(→**8**)
oír decir que	*to hear it said that*	(→**9**)
oír hablar de	*to hear of/about*	(→**10**)
querer decir	*to mean*	(→**11**)

The Perfect Infinitive

- The perfect infinitive is formed using the auxiliary verb **haber** with the past participle of the verb (→**12**)

- The perfect infinitive is found:
  - following certain prepositions, especially **después de** *after* (→**13**)
  - following certain verbal constructions (→**14**)

1 **Al verlo, dejó caer lo que llevaba en las manos**
When he saw him he dropped what he was carrying

2 **Haz entrar a nuestros invitados**
Show our guests in

3 **Quiero hacerles saber que no serán bien recibidos**
I want to let them know that they won't be welcome

4 **Hágale salir, por favor**
Please let him out

5 **Le he hecho venir a Vd porque** ...
I sent for you because ...

6 **Vete a buscar los guantes**
Go and get your gloves

7 **Me he mandado hacer un traje**
I have ordered a suit

8 **Mandaron llamar al médico**
They sent for the doctor

9 **He oído decir que está enfermo**
I've heard it said that he's ill

10 **No he oído hablar más de él**
I haven't heard anything more (said) of him

11 **¿Qué quiere decir eso?**
What does that mean?

12 **haber terminado**   **haberse vestido**
to have finished   to have got dressed

13 **Después de haber comprado el regalo, volvió a casa**
After buying/having bought the present, he went back home
Después de haber madrugado tanto, el taxi se retrasó
After she got up so early, the taxi arrived late

14 **perdonar a alguien por haber hecho**
to forgive somebody for doing/having done
dar las gracias a alguien por haber hecho
to thank somebody for doing/having done
pedir perdón por haber hecho
to be sorry for doing/having done

The Gerund

Formation

- 1st conjugation
  Replace the **-ar** of the infinitive by **-ando** (→**1**)

- 2nd conjugation
  Replace the **-er** of the infinitive by **-iendo** (→**2**)

- 3rd conjugation
  Replace the **-ir** of the infinitive by **-iendo** (→**3**)

- For irregular gerunds, see irregular verbs, p 80 ff.

Uses

- After the verb **estar**, to form the continuous tenses (→**4**)

- After the verbs **seguir** and **continuar** *to continue*, and **ir** when meaning *to happen gradually* (→**5**)

- In time constructions, after **llevar** (→**6**)

- When the action in the main clause needs to be complemented by another action (→**7**)

- The position of object pronouns is the same as for the infinitive (see p 46)

- The gerund is invariable and strictly verbal in sense.

The Present Participle

- It is formed by replacing the **-ar** of the infinitive of 1st conjugation verbs by **-ante**, and the **-er** and **-ir** of the 2nd and 3rd conjugations by **-iente** (→**8**)

- A very limited number of verbs have a present participle, which is either used as an adjective or a noun (→**9/10**)

1 **cantar** → **cantando**
  to sing   singing
2 **temer** → **temiendo**
  to fear   fearing
3 **partir** → **partiendo**
  to leave   leaving
4 **Estoy escribiendo una carta**
  I am writing a letter
  Estaban esperándonos
  They were waiting for us
5 **Sigue viniendo todos los días**
  He/she is still coming every day
  Continuarán subiendo los precios
  Prices will continue to go up
  El ejército iba avanzando poco a poco
  The army was gradually advancing
6 **Lleva dos años estudiando inglés**
  He/she has been studying English for two years
7 **Pasamos el día tomando el sol en la playa**
  We spent the day sunbathing on the beach
  Iba cojeando
  He/she/I was limping
  Salieron corriendo
  They ran out
8 **cantar** → **cantante**
  to sing   singing/singer
  pender → **pendiente**
  to hang   hanging
  seguir → **siguiente**
  to follow   following
9 **agua corriente**
  running water
10 **un estudiante**
  a student

Use of Tenses

The Present

- Unlike English, Spanish often uses the same verb form for the simple present (e.g. *I smoke, he reads, we live*) and the continuous present (e.g. *I am smoking, he is reading, we are living*) (→1)
- Normally, however, the continuous present is used to translate the English:
  to be doing   **estar haciendo** (→2)
- Spanish uses the present tense where English uses the perfect in the following cases:
  - with certain prepositions of time – notably **desde** *for/since* – when an action begun in the past is continued in the present (→3)
    Note, however, that the perfect can be used as in English when the verb is negative (→4)
  - in the construction **acabar de hacer** *to have just done* (→5)
- Like English, Spanish often uses the present where a future action is implied (→6)

The Future

The future is generally used as in English (→7), but note the following:
- Immediate future time is often expressed by means of the present tense of **ir** + **a** + infinitive (→8)
- When 'will' or 'shall' mean 'wish to', 'are willing to', **querer** is used (→9)

The Future Perfect

- Used as in English *shall/will have done* (→10)
- It can also express conjecture, usually about things in the recent past (→11)

Continued

1 **Fumo** I smoke *or* I am smoking
  Lee He reads *or* He is reading
  Vivimos We live *or* We are living
2 **Está fumando**
  He is smoking
3 **Linda estudia español desde hace seis meses**
  Linda's been learning Spanish for six months (*and still is*)
  Estoy de pie desde las siete
  I've been up since seven
  ¿Hace mucho que esperan?
  Have you been waiting long?
  Ya hace dos semanas que estamos aquí
  That's two weeks we've been here (now)
4 **No se han visto desde hace meses**
  They haven't seen each other for months
5 **Isabel acaba de salir**
  Isabel has just left
6 **Mañana voy a Madrid**
  I am going to Madrid tomorrow
7 **Lo haré mañana**
  I'll do it tomorrow
8 **Te vas a caer si no tienes cuidado**
  You'll fall if you're not careful
  Va a perder el tren
  He's going to miss the train
  Va a llevar una media hora
  It'll take about half an hour
9 **¿Me quieres esperar un momento, por favor?**
  Will you wait for me a second, please?
10 **Lo habré acabado para mañana**
  I will have finished it for tomorrow
11 **Ya habrán llegado a casa**
  They must have arrived home by now

Use of Tenses (contd)

The Imperfect
- The imperfect describes:
  - an action or state in the past without definite limits in time (→**1**)
  - habitual action(s) in the past (often expressed in English by means of *would* or *used to*) (→**2**)
- Spanish uses the imperfect tense where English uses the pluperfect in the following cases:
  - with certain prepositions of time – notably **desde** *for/since* – when an action begun in the remoter past was continued in the more recent past (→**3**)

    Note, however, that the pluperfect is used as in English when the verb is negative or the action has been completed (→**4**)
  - in the construction **acabar de hacer** *to have just done* (→**5**)
- Both the continuous and simple forms in English can be translated by the Spanish simple imperfect, but the continuous imperfect is used when the emphasis is on the fact that an action was going on at a precise moment in the past (→**6**)

The Perfect
- The perfect is generally used as in English (→**7**)

The Preterite
- The preterite generally corresponds to the English simple past in both written and spoken Spanish (→**8**)

    However, while English can use the simple past to describe habitual actions or settings, Spanish uses the imperfect (see above) (→**9**)

The Past Anterior
- This tense is only ever used in written, literary Spanish, to replace the pluperfect in time clauses where the verb in the main clause is in the preterite (→**10**)

1 **Todos mirábamos en silencio**
   We were all watching in silence
   Nuestras habitaciones daban a la playa
   Our rooms overlooked the beach

2 **En su juventud se levantaba de madrugada**
   In his youth he got up at dawn
   Hablábamos sin parar durante horas
   We would talk non-stop for hours on end
   Mi hermano siempre me tomaba el pelo
   My brother always used to tease me

3 **Hacía dos años que vivíamos en Irlanda**
   We had been living in Ireland for two years
   Estaba enfermo desde 1990
   He had been ill since 1990
   Hacía mucho tiempo que salían juntos
   They had been going out together for a long time

4 **Hacía un año que no le había visto**
   I hadn't seen him for a year
   Hacía una hora que había llegado
   She had arrived an hour before

5 **Acababa de encontrármelos**
   I had just met them

6 **Cuando llegué, todos estaban fumando**
   When I arrived, they were all smoking

7 **Todavía no han salido**
   They haven't come out yet

8 **Me desperté y salté de la cama**
   I woke up and jumped out of bed

9 **Siempre iban en coche al trabajo**
   They always travelled to work by car

10 **Apenas hubo acabado, se oyeron unos golpes en la puerta**
   She had scarcely finished when there was a knock at the door

The Subjunctive: when to use it

(For how to form the subjunctive see pp 6 ff.)

- After verbs of:
  - 'wishing'
    querer que }
    desear que } to wish that, want (→1)
  - 'emotion' (e.g. regret, surprise, shame, pleasure, etc)
    sentir que   to be sorry that (→2)
    sorprender que   to be surprised that (→3)
    alegrarse de que   to be pleased that (→4)
  - 'asking' and 'advising'
    pedir que   to ask that (→5)
    aconsejar que   to advise that (→6)

In all the above constructions, when the subject of the verbs in the main and subordinate clause is the same, the infinitive is used, and the conjunction **que** omitted (→7)

  - 'ordering', 'forbidding',
    'allowing'
    mandar que* }
    ordenar que* } to order that (→8)
    permitir que* }
    dejar que* } to allow that (→9)
    prohibir que*   to forbid that (→10)
    impedir que*   to prevent that (→11)

*With these verbs either the subjunctive or the infinitive is used when the object of the main verb is the subject of the subordinate verb (→12)

- Always after verbs expressing doubt or uncertainty, and verbs of opinion used negatively
    dudar que   to doubt that (→13)
    no creer que }
    no pensar que } not to think that (→14)

Continued

1 **Queremos que esté contenta**
We want her to be happy (literally: We want that she is happy)
¿Desea Vd que lo haga yo?
Do you want me to do it?

2 **Sentí mucho que no vinieran**
I was very sorry that they didn't come

3 **Nos sorprendió que no les vieran Vds**
We were surprised you didn't see them

4 **Me alegro de que te gusten**
I'm pleased that you like them

5 **Solo les pedimos que tengan cuidado**
We're only asking you to take care

6 **Le aconsejé que no llegara tarde**
I advised him not to be late

7 **Quiero que lo termines pronto**
I want you to finish it soon
but
Quiero terminarlo pronto
I want to finish it soon

8 **Ha mandado que vuelvan**
He has ordered them to come back
Ordenó que fueran castigados
He ordered them to be punished

9 **No permitas que te tomen el pelo**
Don't let them pull your leg
No me dejó que la llevara a casa
She didn't allow me to take her home

10 **Te prohíbo que digas eso**
I forbid you to say that

11 **No les impido que vengan**
I am not preventing them from coming

12 **Les ordenó que salieran** *or* **Les ordenó salir**
She ordered them to go out

13 **Dudo que lo sepan hacer**
I doubt they can do it

14 **No creo que sean tan listos**
I don't think they are as clever as that

The Subjunctive: when to use it (contd)

- In impersonal constructions which express necessity, possibility, etc

  hace falta que
  es necesario que } *it is necessary that* (→**1**)
  es posible que   *it is possible that* (→**2**)
  más vale que   *it is better that* (→**3**)
  es una lástima que   *it is a pity that* (→**4**)

  Note that in impersonal constructions which state a fact or express certainty the indicative is used when the impersonal verb is affirmative. When it is negative, the subjunctive is used (→**5**)

- After certain conjunctions

  para que
  a fin de que* } *so that* (→**6**)
  como si   *as if* (→**7**)
  sin que*   *without* (→**8**)
  a condición de que*
  con tal (de) que* } *provided that,*
  siempre que   *on condition that* (→**9**)
  a menos que
  a no ser que } *unless* (→**10**)
  antes (de) que*   *before* (→**11**)
  no sea que   *lest/in case* (→**12**)
  mientras (que)
  siempre que } *as long as* (→**13**)
  (el) que   *the fact that* (→**14**)

*When the subject of both verbs is the same, the infinitive is used, and the final **que** is omitted (→**8**)

Continued

1 **¿Hace falta que vaya Jaime?**
Does James have to go?
2 **Es posible que tengan razón**
It's possible that they are right
3 **Más vale que se quede Vd en su casa**
It's better that you stay at home
4 **Es una lástima que haya perdido su perrito**
It's a shame/pity that she has lost her puppy
5 **Es verdad que va a venir**
It's true that he's coming
but
No es verdad que vayan a hacerlo
It's not true that they are going to do it
6 **Átalas bien para que no se caigan**
Tie them up tightly so that they won't fall
7 **Hablaba como si no creyera en sus propias palabras**
He talked as if he didn't believe in his own words
8 **Salimos sin que nos vieran**
We left without them seeing us
but
Me fui sin esperarla
I went without waiting for her
9 **Lo haré con tal de que me cuentes todo lo que pasó**
I'll do it provided you tell me all that happened
10 **Saldremos de paseo a menos que esté lloviendo**
We'll go for a walk unless it's raining
11 **Avísale antes de que sea demasiado tarde**
Warn him before it's too late
12 **Habla en voz baja, no sea que alguien nos oiga**
Speak softly in case anyone hears us
13 **Eso no pasará mientras yo sea el jefe aquí**
That won't happen as long as I am the boss here
14 **El que no me escribiera no me importaba demasiado**
The fact that he didn't write didn't matter to me too much

The Subjunctive: when to use it (contd)

- After the conjunctions
  de modo que
  de forma que } *so that* (indicating a purpose) (→1)
  de manera que

Note that when these conjunctions introduce a result and not a purpose the subjunctive is not used (→2)

- In relative clauses with an antecedent which is:
  – negative (→3)
  – indefinite (→4)
  – non-specific (→5)

- In main clauses, to express a wish or exhortation. The verb may be preceded by expressions like **ojalá** or **que** (→6)

- In the **si** clause of conditions where the English sentence contains a conditional tense (→7)

- In set expressions (→8)

- In the following constructions which translate *however*:
  – **por** + adjective + subjunctive (→9)
  – **por** + adverb + subjunctive (→10)
  – **por** + **mucho** + subjunctive (→11)

Continued

1 **Vuélvanse** de manera que **les vea bien**
Turn round so that I can see you properly

2 **No quieren hacerlo,** de manera que **tendré** que hacerlo yo
They won't do it, so I'll have to do it myself

3 No **he encontrado a nadie que** la **conociera**
I haven't met anyone who knows her
No **dijo nada que no supiéramos ya**
He/she didn't say anything we didn't already know

4 **Necesito alguien que sepa conducir**
I need someone who can drive
Busco algo que me distraiga
I'm looking for something to take my mind off it

5 **Busca una casa que tenga calefacción central**
He/she's looking for a house which has central heating
(*subjunctive used since such a house may or may not exist*)
El que lo haya visto tiene que decírmelo
Anyone who has seen it must tell me
(*subjunctive used since it is not known who has seen it*)

6 **¡Ojalá haga buen tiempo!**
Let's hope the weather will be good!
¡Que te diviertas!
Have a good time!

7 **Si fuéramos en coche llegaríamos a tiempo**
If we went by car we'd be there in time

8 **Diga lo que diga** ...   **Sea lo que sea** ...
Whatever he may say ...   Be that as it may ...
Pase lo que pase ...   **Sea como sea** ...
Come what may ... ·   One way or another ...

9 **Por cansado que esté, seguirá trabajando**
No matter how/however tired he may be, he'll go on working

10 **Por lejos que viva, iremos a buscarle**
No matter how/however far away he lives, we'll go and look for him

11 **Por mucho que lo intente, nunca lo conseguirá**
No matter how/however hard he tries, he'll never succeed

The Subjunctive (contd)

Clauses taking either a subjunctive or an indicative

In certain constructions, a subjunctive is needed when the action refers to future events or hypothetical situations, whereas an indicative is used when stating a fact or experience (→1)

The commonest of these are:
- The conjunctions

cuando	*when* (→1)
en cuanto **tan pronto como**	} *as soon as* (→2)
después (de) que*	*after* (→3)
hasta que	*until* (→4)
mientras	*while* (→5)
siempre que	*whenever* (→6)
aunque	*even though* (→7)

all conjunctions and pronouns ending in **-quiera** (-*ever*) (→8)

*Note that if the subject of both verbs is the same, the subjunctive introduced by **después (de) que** may be replaced by **después de** + infinitive (→9)

Sequence of tenses in Subordinate Clauses

- If the verb in the main clause is in the present, future or imperative, the verb in the dependent clause will be in the present or perfect subjunctive (→10)

- If the verb in the main clause is in the conditional or any past tense, the verb in the dependent clause will be in the imperfect or pluperfect subjunctive (→11)

1 **Le aconsejé que** oyera **música** cuando estuviera **nervioso**
   I advised him to listen to music when he felt nervous
   Me gusta nadar cuando hace **calor**
   I like to swim when it is warm

2 **Te devolveré el libro** tan pronto como lo haya leído
   I'll give you back the book as soon as I have read it

3 **Te lo diré** después de que **te** hayas **sentado**
   I'll tell you after you've sat down

4 **Quédate aquí** hasta que volvamos
   Stay here until we come back

5 **No hablen en voz alta** mientras estén **ellos aquí**
   Don't speak loudly while they are here

6 **Vuelvan por aquí** siempre que quieran
   Come back whenever you wish to

7 **No le creeré** aunque diga **la verdad**
   I won't believe him even if he tells the truth

8 **La encontraré** dondequiera **que** esté
   I will find her wherever she might be

9 **Después de cenar** nos fuimos al cine
   After dinner we went to the cinema

10 Quiero **que lo** hagas (*pres + pres subj*)
   I want you to do it
   Temo **que no** haya **venido** (*pres + perf subj*)
   I fear he hasn't come (might not have come)
   Iremos **por aquí para que no nos** vean (*future + pres subj*)
   We'll go this way so that they won't see us

11 **Me** gustaría **que** llegaras **temprano** (*cond + imperf subj*)
   I'd like you to arrive early
   Les pedí **que me** esperaran (*preterite + imperf subj*)
   I asked them to wait for me
   Sentiría **mucho que** hubiese **muerto** (*cond + pluperf subj*)
   I would be very sorry if he were dead

Verbs governing a, de, con, en, por and para

The following lists (pp 66 to 73) contain common verbal constructions using the prepositions **a, de, con, en, por** and **para**.

Note the following abbreviations:

infin	infinitive
perf infin	perfect infinitive*
algn	alguien
sb	somebody
sth	something

*For formation see p 50

aburrirse de + infin	*to get bored with doing* (→1)
acabar con algo/algn	*to put an end to sth/finish with sb* (→2)
acabar de* + infin	*to have just done* (→3)
acabar por + infin	*to end up doing* (→4)
acercarse a algo/algn	*to approach sth/sb*
acordarse de algo/algn/de + infin	*to remember sth/sb/doing* (→5)
acostumbrarse a algo/algn/a + infin	*to get used to sth/sb/to doing* (→6)
acusar a algn de algo/de + perf infin	*to accuse sb of sth/of doing, having done* (→7)
advertir a algn de algo	*to notify, warn sb about sth* (→8)
aficionarse a algo/a + infin	*to grow fond of sth/of doing* (→9)
alegrarse de algo/de + perf infin	*to be glad about sth/of doing, having done* (→10)
alejarse de algn/algo	*to move away from sb/sth*
amenazar a algn con algo/con + infin	*to threaten sb with sth/to do* (→11)
animar a algn a + infin	*to encourage sb to do*
apresurarse a + infin	*to hurry to do* (→12)

*See also Use of Tenses, pp 54 and 56

Continued

1 **Me aburría de no poder salir de casa**
I used to get bored with not being able to leave the house

2 **Quiso acabar con su vida**
He wanted to put an end to his life

3 **Acababan de llegar cuando ...**
They had just arrived when ...

4 **El acusado acabó por confesarlo todo**
The accused ended up by confessing everything

5 **Nos acordamos muy bien de aquellas vacaciones**
We remember that holiday very well

6 **Me he acostumbrado a levantarme temprano**
I've got used to getting up early

7 **Le acusó de haber mentido**
She accused him of lying

8 **Advertí a mi amigo del peligro que corría**
I warned my friend about the danger he was in

9 **Nos hemos aficionado a la música clásica**
We've grown fond of classical music

10 **Me alegro de haberle conocido**
I'm glad I met him

11 **Amenazó con denunciarles**
He threatened to report them

12 **Se apresuraron a coger sitio**
They hurried to find a seat

Verbs governing a, de, con, en, por and para (contd)

aprender a + infin	*to learn to do* (→1)
aprovecharse de algo/algn	*to take advantage of sth/sb*
aproximarse a algn/algo	*to approach sb/sth*
asistir a algo	*to attend sth, be at sth*
asomarse a/por	*to lean out of* (→2)
asombrarse de + infin	*to be surprised at doing* (→3)
atreverse a + infin	*to dare to do*
avergonzarse de algo/algn/de + perf infin	*to be ashamed of sth/sb/of doing, having done* (→4)
ayudar a algn a + infin	*to help sb to do* (→5)
bajarse de (+ place/vehicle)	*to get off/out of* (→6)
burlarse de algn	*to make fun of sb*
cansarse de algo/algn/de + infin	*to tire of sth/sb/of doing*
carecer de algo	*to lack sth* (→7)
cargar de algo	*to load with sth* (→8)
casarse con algn	*to get married to sb* (→9)
cesar de + infin	*to stop doing*
chocar con algo	*to crash/bump into sth* (→10)
comenzar a + infin	*to begin to do*
comparar con algn/algo	*to compare with sb/sth*
consentir en + infin	*to agree to do*
consistir en + infin	*to consist of doing* (→11)
constar de algo	*to consist of sth* (→12)
contar con algn/algo	*to rely on sb/sth* (→13)
convenir en + infin	*to agree to do* (→14)
darse cuenta de algo	*to realise sth*
dejar de + infin	*to stop doing* (→15)
depender de algo/algn	*to depend on sth/sb* (→16)
despedirse de algn	*to say goodbye to sb*
dirigirse a + place/**a algn**	*to head for/address sb*
disponerse a + infin	*to get ready to do*
empezar a + infin	*to begin to do*
empezar por + infin	*to begin by doing* (→17)

Continued

1 **Me gustaría** aprender a nadar
   I'd like to learn to swim
2 **No** te asomes a **la ventana**
   Don't lean out of the window
3 Nos asombramos **mucho** de verles ahí
   We were very surprised at seeing them there
4 **No** me avergüenzo de haberlo hecho
   I'm not ashamed of having done it
5 Ayúdeme a llevar **estas maletas**
   Help me to carry these cases
6 Se bajó del coche
   He got out of the car
7 **La casa** carecía de jardín
   The house lacked (did not have) a garden
8 **El carro iba** cargado de paja
   The cart was loaded with straw
9 Se casó con Andrés
   She married Andrew
10 **Enciende la luz, o** chocarás con la puerta
   Turn the light on, or you'll bump into the door
11 **Mi plan** consistía en vigilarles de cerca
   My plan consisted of keeping a close eye on them
12 **El examen** consta de **tres** partes
   The exam consists of three parts
13 Cuento contigo **para que me ayudes a hacerlo**
   I rely on you to help me do it
14 Convinieron en reunir**se al día siguiente**
   They agreed to meet the following day
15 **¿Quieres** dejar de hablar**?**
   Will you stop talking?
16 **No** depende de mí
   It doesn't depend on me
17 Empieza por enterar**te de lo que se trata**
   Begin by finding out what it is about

Verbs governing a, de, con, en, por and para (contd)

encontrarse con algn	*to meet sb (by chance)* ($\rightarrow$1)
enfadarse con algn	*to get annoyed with sb*
enseñar a algn a + infin	*to teach sb to* ($\rightarrow$2)
enterarse de algo	*to find out about sth* ($\rightarrow$3)
entrar en (+ place)	*to enter, go into*
esperar a + infin	*to wait until* ($\rightarrow$4)
estar de acuerdo con algn/ algo	*to agree with sb/sth*
fiarse de algn/algo	*to trust sb/sth*
fijarse en algo/algn	*to notice sth/sb* ($\rightarrow$5)
hablar con algn	*to talk to sb* ($\rightarrow$6)
hacer caso a algn	*to pay attention to sb*
hartarse de algo/algn/de + infin	*to get fed up with sth/sb/with doing* ($\rightarrow$7)
interesarse por algo/algn	*to be interested in sth/sb* ($\rightarrow$8)
invitar a algn a + infin	*to invite sb to do*
jugar a (+ sports, games)	*to play*
luchar por algo/por + infin	*to fight, strive for/to do* ($\rightarrow$9)
llegar a (+ place)/a + infin	*to reach/to manage to do* ($\rightarrow$10)
llenar de algo	*to fill with sth*
negarse a + infin	*to refuse to do* ($\rightarrow$11)
obligar a algn a + infin	*to make sb do* ($\rightarrow$12)
ocuparse de algn/algo	*to take care of sb/attend to sth*
oler a algo	*to smell of sth* ($\rightarrow$13)
olvidarse de algo/algn/de + infin	*to forget sth/sb/to do* ($\rightarrow$14)
oponerse a algo/a + infin	*to be opposed to sth/to doing*
parecerse a algn/algo	*to resemble sb/sth*
pensar en algo/algn/en + infin	*to think about sth/sb/about doing* ($\rightarrow$15)
preguntar por algn	*to ask for/about sb*
preocuparse de or por algo/ algn	*to worry about sth/sb* ($\rightarrow$16)

Continued

1 Me encontré con ella **al entrar en el Banco**
  I met her as I was entering the Bank
2 Le estoy enseñando a nadar
  I am teaching him to swim
3 ¿Te has enterado del sitio **adonde hay que ir?**
  Have you found out where we have to go?
4 Espera a saber **lo que quiere antes de comprar el regalo**
  Wait until you know what he wants before buying the present
5 Me fijé en él **cuando subía a su coche**
  I noticed him when he was getting into his car
6 ¿**Puedo** hablar con Vd **un momento?**
  May I talk to you for a moment?
7 Me he hartado de escribir**le**
  I've got fed up with writing to him
8 Me interesaba **mucho** por la arqueología
  I was very interested in archaeology
9 **Hay que** luchar por mantener **la paz**
  One must strive to preserve peace
10 **Lo intenté sin** llegar a conseguir**lo**
  I tried without managing to do it
11 **Se** negó a hacer**lo**
  He refused to do it
12 Le obligó a sentar**se**
  He made him sit down
13 **Este perfume** huele a jazmín
  This perfume smells of jasmine
14 **Siempre** me olvido de cerrar **la puerta**
  I always forget to shut the door
15 **No quiero** pensar en eso
  I don't want to think about that
16 Se preocupa **mucho** de/por **su** apariencia
  He worries a lot about his appearance

Verbs governing a, de, con, en, por and para (contd)

prepararse a + infin	*to prepare to do*
probar a + infin	*to try to do*
quedar en + infin	*to agree to do* (→1)
quedar por + infin	*to remain to be done* (→2)
quejarse de algo	*to complain of sth*
referirse a algo	*to refer to sth*
reírse de algo/algn	*to laugh at sth/sb*
rodear de	*to surround with* (→3)
romper a + infin	*to (suddenly) start to do* (→4)
salir de (+ place)	*to leave*
sentarse a (+ table etc)	*to sit down at*
subir(se) a (+ vehicle/place)	*to get on, into/to climb* (→5)
servir de algo a algn	*to be useful to/serve sb as sth* (→6)
servir para algo/para + infin	*to be good as sth/for doing* (→7)
servirse de algo	*to use sth* (→8)
soñar con algn/algo/con + infin	*to dream about/of sb/sth/of doing*
sorprenderse de algo	*to be surprised at sth*
tardar en + infin	*to take time to do* (→9)
tener ganas de algo/de + infin	*to want sth/to do* (→10)
tener miedo de algo	*to be afraid of sth* (→11)
tener miedo a algn	*to be afraid of sb* (→12)
terminar por + infin	*to end by doing*
tirar de algo/algn	*to pull sth/sb*
trabajar de (+ occupation)	*to work as* (→13)
trabajar en (+ place of work)	*to work at/in* (→14)
traducir a (+ language)	*to translate into*
tratar de + infin	*to try to do* (→15)
tratarse de algo/algn/de + infin	*to be a question of sth/about sb/about doing* (→16)
vacilar en + infin	*to hesitate to do* (→17)
volver a + infin	*to do again* (→18)

1 **Habíamos** quedado en encontrar**nos a las 8**
We had agreed to meet at 8

2 Queda por averiguar **dónde se ocultan**
It remains to be discovered where they are hiding

3 Habían rodeado **el jardín** de **un seto de cipreses**
They had surrounded the garden with a hedge of cypress trees

4 **Al apagarse la luz, el niño** rompió a llorar
When the lights went out, the little boy suddenly started to cry

5 ¡**De prisa,** sube al coche!
Get into the car, quick!

6 **Esto** me servirá de bastón
This will serve me as a walking stick

7 **No** sirvo para (ser) jardinero
I'm no good as a gardener

8 Se sirvió de **un** destornillador **para abrirlo**
She used a screwdriver to open it

9 Tardaron **mucho** en salir
They took a long time to come out

10 Tengo ganas de volver **a España**
I want to go back to Spain

11 **Mi hija** tiene miedo de **la** oscuridad
My daughter is afraid of the dark

12 **Nunca** tuvieron miedo a **su** padre
They were never afraid of their father

13 **Pedro** trabaja de camarero **en Londres**
Peter works as a waiter in London

14 Trabajaba en **una** oficina
I used to work in an office

15 **No** trates de engañar**me**
Don't try to fool me

16 Se trata de **nuestro nuevo** vecino
It's about our new neighbour

17 **Nunca** vacilaban en pedir **dinero**
They never hesitated to borrow money

18 **No** vuelvas a hacer**lo nunca más**
Don't ever do it again

Ser and Estar

Spanish has two verbs — **ser** and **estar** — for *to be*.
They are not interchangeable and each one is used in defined contexts.

ser is used:

- With an adjective, to express a permanent or inherent quality (→1)
- To express occupation or nationality (→2)
- To express possession (→3)
- To express origin or the material from which something is made (→4)
- With a noun, pronoun or infinitive following the verb (→5)
- To express the time and date (→6)
- To form the passive, with the past participle (see p 32).
  Note that this use emphasizes the action of the verb. If, however, the resultant state or condition needs to be emphasized, **estar** is used. The past participle then functions as an adjective (see p 204) and has to agree in gender and in number with the noun (→7)

estar is used:

- Always, to indicate place or location (→8)
- With an adjective or adjectival phrase, to express a quality or state seen by the speaker as subject to change or different from expected (→9)
- When speaking of a person's state of health (→10)
- To form the continuous tenses, used with the gerund (see p 52) (→11)
- With **de** + noun, to indicate a temporary occupation (→12)

Continued

1 **Mi hermano** es alto   **María** es inteligente
   My brother is tall   Mary is intelligent

2 **Javier** es aviador   **Sus padres** son italianos
   Javier is an airman   His parents are Italian

3 **La casa** es de Miguel
   The house belongs to Michael

4 **Mi hermana** es de Granada   **Las paredes** son de ladrillo
   My sister is from Granada   The walls are made of brick

5 **Andrés** es **un** niño **travieso**
   Andrew is a naughty boy
   Soy yo, Enrique
   It's me, Henry
   Todo es proponér**selo**
   It's all a question of putting your mind to it

6 Son las tres y media   Mañana es sábado
   It's half past three   Tomorrow is Saturday

7 **Las puertas** eran cerradas **sigilosamente**
   The doors were being silently closed
   Las puertas estaban cerradas
   The doors were closed
   (*resultant action*)

8 **La comida** está en la mesa
   The meal is on the table

9 **Su amigo** está enfermo   **El lavabo** está ocupado
   Her friend is ill   The toilet is engaged
   Hoy estoy de mal humor   **Las tiendas** están cerradas
   I'm in a bad mood today   The shops are closed

10 ¿Cómo están **Vds?**   Estamos **todos** bien
   How are you?   We are all well

11 Estamos aprendiendo **mucho**
   We are learning a great deal

12 **Mi primo** está de médico **en un pueblo**
   My cousin works as a doctor in a village

Ser and Estar (contd)

With certain adjectives, both **ser** and **estar** can be used, although they are not interchangeable when used in this way:
  — **ser** will express a permanent or inherent quality (→1)
  — **estar** will express a temporary state or quality (→2)

Both **ser** and **estar** may also be used in set expressions.

The commonest of these are:
● With **ser**

Sea como sea	*Be that as it may*
Es igual/Es lo mismo	*It's all the same*
llegar a ser	*to become*
¿Cómo fue eso?	*How did that happen?*
¿Qué ha sido de él?	*What has become of him?*
ser para (with the idea of purpose)	*to be for* (→3)

● With **estar**

estar de pie/de rodillas	*to be standing/kneeling*
estar de viaje	*to be travelling*
estar de vacaciones	*to be on holiday*
estar de vuelta	*to be back*
estar de moda	*to be in fashion*
Está bien	*It's all right*
estar para	*to be about to do sth/to be in a mood for* (→4)
estar por	*to be inclined to/to be (all) for* (→5)
estar a punto de	*to be just about to do sth* (→6)

Continued

1 **Su hermana** es **muy** joven/vieja
His sister is very young/old
Son **muy** ricos/pobres
They are very rich/poor
Su amigo era un enfermo
His friend was an invalid
Es un borracho
He is a drunkard
Mi hijo es bueno/malo
My son is good/naughty
Viajar es cansado
Travelling is tiring

2 Está **muy** joven/vieja con ese vestido
She looks very young/old in that dress
Ahora están **muy** ricos/pobres
They have become very rich/poor lately
Estaba enfermo
He was ill
Está borracho
He is drunk
Está bueno/malo
He is well/ill
Hoy estoy cansada
I am tired today

3 **Este paquete** es para **Vd**
This parcel is for you
Esta caja es para **guardar semillas**
This box is for keeping seeds in

4 **Están para** llegar
They're about to arrive

5 **Estoy por** irme a vivir a España
I'm inclined to go and live in Spain

6 **Las rosas** están a punto de **salir**
The roses are about to come out

Verbal Idioms

Special Intransitive Verbs

With the following verbs the Spanish construction is the opposite of the English. The subject in English becomes the indirect object of the Spanish verb, while the object in English becomes the subject of the Spanish verb.

Compare the following:

I like that house (subject: *I*, object: *that house*)

Esa casa me gusta (subject: **esa casa**, indirect object: **me**)

The commonest of these verbs are:

gustar	*to like* (→1)
gustar más	*to prefer* (→2)
encantar	(colloquial) *to love* (→3)
faltar	*to need/to be short of/to have missing* (→4)
quedar	*to be/have left* (→5)
doler	*to have a pain in/to hurt, ache* (→6)
interesar	*to be interested in* (→7)
importar	*to mind* (→8)

1 **Me gusta este vestido**
I like this dress (This dress pleases me)

2 **Me gustan más éstas**
I prefer these

3 **Nos encanta hacer deporte**
We love sport

4 **Me faltaban 100 pesetas**
I was short of 100 pesetas
Sólo le falta el toque final
It just needs the finishing touch
Le faltaban tres dientes
He/she had three teeth missing

5 **Sólo nos quedan dos kilómetros**
We only have two kilometres (left) to go

6 **Me duele la cabeza**
I have a headache

7 **Nos interesa mucho la política**
We are very interested in politics

8 **No me importa la lluvia**
I don't mind the rain

Irregular Verbs

The verbs listed opposite and conjugated on pp 82 to 161 provide the main patterns for irregular verbs. The verbs are grouped opposite according to their infinitive ending and are shown in the following tables in alphabetical order. All pronouns are shown in colour. Colour is also used to help identify verb endings and irregular forms.

In the tables, the most important irregular verbs are given in their most common simple tenses, together with the imperative and the gerund.

The past participle is also shown for each verb, to enable you to form all the compound tenses, as on pp 18 to 23.

The pronouns **ella** and **Vd** take the same verb endings as **él**, while **ellas** and **Vds** take the same endings as **ellos**.

- All the verbs included in the tables differ from the three conjugations set out on pp 8 to 13. Many — e.g. **contar** — serve as models for groups of verbs, while others — e.g. **ir** — are unique. On pp 162 to 186 you will find over 2,800 commonly used verbs listed alphabetically and cross-referred either to the relevant basic conjugation or to the appropriate model in the verb tables.

'-ar':
- actuar
- almorzar
- andar
- aunar
- avergonzar
- averiguar
- contar
- cruzar
- dar
- empezar
- enviar
- errar
- estar
- jugar
- negar
- pagar
- pensar
- rehusar
- rogar
- sacar
- volcar

'-er':
- caber
- caer
- cocer
- coger
- crecer
- entender
- haber
- hacer
- hay
- leer
- llover
- mover
- nacer
- oler
- poder
- poner
- querer
- resolver
- romper

'-er':
- saber
- satisfacer
- ser
- tener
- torcer
- traer
- valer
- vencer
- ver
- volver

'-ir':
- abolir
- abrir
- adquirir
- bendecir
- conducir
- construir
- cubrir
- decir
- dirigir
- distinguir
- dormir
- elegir
- erguir
- escribir
- freír
- gruñir
- ir
- lucir
- morir
- oír
- pedir
- prohibir
- reír
- reñir
- reunir
- salir
- seguir
- sentir
- venir
- zurcir

abolir *to abolish*

PAST PARTICIPLE
abolido

IMPERATIVE
abolid

GERUND
aboliendo

PRESENT		*PRESENT SUBJUNCTIVE*
*		*not used*
nosotros	abolimos	
vosotros	abolís	

FUTURE		*CONDITIONAL*	
yo	aboliré	yo	aboliría
tú	abolirás	tú	abolirías
él	abolirá	él	aboliría
nosotros	aboliremos	nosotros	aboliríamos
vosotros	aboliréis	vosotros	aboliríais
ellos	abolirán	ellos	abolirían

IMPERFECT		*PRETERITE*	
yo	abolía	yo	abolí
tú	abolías	tú	aboliste
él	abolía	él	abolió
nosotros	abolíamos	nosotros	abolimos
vosotros	abolíais	vosotros	abolisteis
ellos	abolían	ellos	abolieron

---

*present tense only used in persons shown

abrir *to open*

PAST PARTICIPLE
abierto

GERUND
abriendo

IMPERATIVE
abre
abrid

PRESENT
yo	abro
tú	abres
él	abre
nosotros	abrimos
vosotros	abrís
ellos	abren

FUTURE
yo	abriré
tú	abrirás
él	abrirá
nosotros	abriremos
vosotros	abriréis
ellos	abrirán

IMPERFECT
yo	abría
tú	abrías
él	abría
nosotros	abríamos
vosotros	abríais
ellos	abrían

PRESENT SUBJUNCTIVE
yo	abra
tú	abras
él	abra
nosotros	abramos
vosotros	abráis
ellos	abran

CONDITIONAL
yo	abriría
tú	abrirías
él	abriría
nosotros	abriríamos
vosotros	abriríais
ellos	abrirían

PRETERITE
yo	abrí
tú	abriste
él	abrió
nosotros	abrimos
vosotros	abristeis
ellos	abrieron

actuar *to act*

PAST PARTICIPLE
actuado

GERUND
actuando

IMPERATIVE
actúa
actuad

PRESENT			*PRESENT SUBJUNCTIVE*	
yo	actúo		yo	actúe
tú	actúas		tú	actúes
él	actúa		él	actúe
nosotros	actuamos		nosotros	actuemos
vosotros	actuáis		vosotros	actuéis
ellos	actúan		ellos	actúen

FUTURE			*CONDITIONAL*	
yo	actuaré		yo	actuaría
tú	actuarás		tú	actuarías
él	actuará		él	actuaría
nosotros	actuaremos		nosotros	actuaríamos
vosotros	actuaréis		vosotros	actuaríais
ellos	actuarán		ellos	actuarían

IMPERFECT			*PRETERITE*	
yo	actuaba		yo	actué
tú	actuabas		tú	actuaste
él	actuaba		él	actuó
nosotros	actuábamos		nosotros	actuamos
vosotros	actuabais		vosotros	actuasteis
ellos	actuaban		ellos	actuaron

adquirir *to acquire*

PAST PARTICIPLE
adquirido

IMPERATIVE
adquiere
adquirid

GERUND
adquiriendo

PRESENT

yo	adquiero
tú	adquieres
él	adquiere
nosotros	adquirimos
vosotros	adquirís
ellos	adquieren

PRESENT SUBJUNCTIVE

yo	adquiera
tú	adquieras
él	adquiera
nosotros	adquiramos
vosotros	adquiráis
ellos	adquieran

FUTURE

yo	adquiriré
tú	adquirirás
él	adquirirá
nosotros	adquiriremos
vosotros	adquiriréis
ellos	adquirirán

CONDITIONAL

yo	adquiriría
tú	adquirirías
él	adquiriría
nosotros	adquiriríamos
vosotros	adquiriríais
ellos	adquirirían

IMPERFECT

yo	adquiría
tú	adquirías
él	adquiría
nosotros	adquiríamos
vosotros	adquiríais
ellos	adquirían

PRETERITE

yo	adquirí
tú	adquiriste
él	adquirió
nosotros	adquirimos
vosotros	adquiristeis
ellos	adquirieron

almorzar *to have lunch*

PAST PARTICIPLE
  almorzado

IMPERATIVE
  almuerza
  almorzad

GERUND
  almorzando

PRESENT
yo	almuerzo
tú	almuerzas
él	almuerza
nosotros	almorzamos
vosotros	almorzáis
ellos	almuerzan

FUTURE
yo	almorzaré
tú	almorzarás
él	almorzará
nosotros	almorzaremos
vosotros	almorzaréis
ellos	almorzarán

IMPERFECT
yo	almorzaba
tú	almorzabas
él	almorzaba
nosotros	almorzábamos
vosotros	almorzabais
ellos	almorzaban

PRESENT SUBJUNCTIVE
yo	almuerce
tú	almuerces
él	almuerce
nosotros	almorcemos
vosotros	almorcéis
ellos	almuercen

CONDITIONAL
yo	almorzaría
tú	almorzarías
él	almorzaría
nosotros	almorzaríamos
vosotros	almorzaríais
ellos	almorzarían

PRETERITE
yo	almorcé
tú	almorzaste
él	almorzó
nosotros	almorzamos
vosotros	almorzasteis
ellos	almorzaron

andar *to walk*

PAST PARTICIPLE
andado

GERUND
andando

IMPERATIVE
anda
andad

PRESENT

yo	ando
tú	andas
él	anda
nosotros	andamos
vosotros	andáis
ellos	andan

FUTURE

yo	andaré
tú	andarás
él	andará
nosotros	andaremos
vosotros	andaréis
ellos	andarán

IMPERFECT

yo	andaba
tú	andabas
él	andaba
nosotros	andábamos
vosotros	andabais
ellos	andaban

PRESENT SUBJUNCTIVE

yo	ande
tú	andes
él	ande
nosotros	andemos
vosotros	andéis
ellos	anden

CONDITIONAL

yo	andaría
tú	andarías
él	andaría
nosotros	andaríamos
vosotros	andaríais
ellos	andarían

PRETERITE

yo	anduve
tú	anduviste
él	anduvo
nosotros	anduvimos
vosotros	anduvisteis
ellos	anduvieron

aunar *to join together*

PAST PARTICIPLE
aunado

GERUND
aunando

IMPERATIVE
aúna
aunad

PRESENT

yo	aúno
tú	aúnas
él	aúna
nosotros	aunamos
vosotros	aunáis
ellos	aúnan

FUTURE

yo	aunaré
tú	aunarás
él	aunará
nosotros	aunaremos
vosotros	aunaréis
ellos	aunarán

IMPERFECT

yo	aunaba
tú	aunabas
él	aunaba
nosotros	aunábamos
vosotros	aunabais
ellos	aunaban

PRESENT SUBJUNCTIVE

yo	aúne
tú	aúnes
él	aúne
nosotros	aunemos
vosotros	aunéis
ellos	aúnen

CONDITIONAL

yo	aunaría
tú	aunarías
él	aunaría
nosotros	aunaríamos
vosotros	aunaríais
ellos	aunarían

PRETERITE

yo	auné
tú	aunaste
él	aunó
nosotros	aunamos
vosotros	aunasteis
ellos	aunaron

avergonzar *to shame*

PAST PARTICIPLE
avergonzado

GERUND
avergonzando

IMPERATIVE
avergüenza
avergonzad

PRESENT

yo	avergüenzo
tú	avergüenzas
él	avergüenza
nosotros	avergonzamos
vosotros	avergonzáis
ellos	avergüenzan

FUTURE

yo	avergonzaré
tú	avergonzarás
él	avergonzará
nosotros	avergonzaremos
vosotros	avergonzaréis
ellos	avergonzarán

IMPERFECT

yo	avergonzaba
tú	avergonzabas
él	avergonzaba
nosotros	avergonzábamos
vosotros	avergonzabais
ellos	avergonzaban

PRESENT SUBJUNCTIVE

yo	avergüence
tú	avergüences
él	avergüence
nosotros	avergoncemos
vosotros	avergoncéis
ellos	avergüencen

CONDITIONAL

yo	avergonzaría
tú	avergonzarías
él	avergonzaría
nosotros	avergonzaríamos
vosotros	avergonzaríais
ellos	avergonzarían

PRETERITE

yo	avergoncé
tú	avergonzaste
él	avergonzó
nosotros	avergonzamos
vosotros	avergonzasteis
ellos	avergonzaron

averiguar *to find out*

PAST PARTICIPLE
averigu**ado**

GERUND
averigu**ando**

IMPERATIVE
averigu**a**
averigu**ad**

PRESENT
yo	averigu**o**
tú	averigu**as**
él	averigu**a**
nosotros	averigu**amos**
vosotros	averigu**áis**
ellos	averigu**an**

PRESENT SUBJUNCTIVE
yo	averig**üe**
tú	averig**ües**
él	averg**üe**
nosotros	averig**üemos**
vosotros	averig**üéis**
ellos	averig**üen**

FUTURE
yo	averiguar**é**
tú	averiguar**ás**
él	averiguar**á**
nosotros	averiguar**emos**
vosotros	averiguar**éis**
ellos	averiguar**án**

CONDITIONAL
yo	averiguar**ía**
tú	averiguar**ías**
él	averiguar**ía**
nosotros	averiguar**íamos**
vosotros	averiguar**íais**
ellos	averiguar**ían**

IMPERFECT
yo	averigu**aba**
tú	averigu**abas**
él	averigu**aba**
nosotros	averigu**ábamos**
vosotros	averigu**abais**
ellos	averigu**aban**

PRETERITE
yo	averig**üé**
tú	averigu**aste**
él	averigu**ó**
nosotros	averigu**amos**
vosotros	averigu**asteis**
ellos	averigu**aron**

bendecir *to bless*

PAST PARTICIPLE
bendecido

GERUND
bendiciendo

IMPERATIVE
bendice
bendecid

PRESENT		PRESENT SUBJUNCTIVE	
yo	bendigo	yo	bendiga
tú	bendices	tú	bendigas
él	bendice	él	bendiga
nosotros	bendecimos	nosotros	bendigamos
vosotros	bendecís	vosotros	bendigáis
ellos	bendicen	ellos	bendigan

FUTURE		CONDITIONAL	
yo	bendeciré	yo	bendeciría
tú	bendecirás	tú	bendecirías
él	bendecirá	él	bendeciría
nosotros	bendeciremos	nosotros	bendeciríamos
vosotros	bendeciréis	vosotros	bendeciríais
ellos	bendecirán	ellos	bendecirían

IMPERFECT		PRETERITE	
yo	bendecía	yo	bendije
tú	bendecías	tú	bendijiste
él	bendecía	él	bendijo
nosotros	bendecíamos	nosotros	bendijimos
vosotros	bendecíais	vosotros	bendijisteis
ellos	bendecían	ellos	bendijeron

caber *to fit*

PAST PARTICIPLE
cabido

GERUND
cabiendo

IMPERATIVE
cabe
cabed

PRESENT		*PRESENT SUBJUNCTIVE*	
yo	quepo	yo	quepa
tú	cabes	tú	quepas
él	cabe	él	quepa
nosotros	cabemos	nosotros	quepamos
vosotros	cabéis	vosotros	quepáis
ellos	caben	ellos	quepan

FUTURE		*CONDITIONAL*	
yo	cabré	yo	cabría
tú	cabrás	tú	cabrías
él	cabrá	él	cabría
nosotros	cabremos	nosotros	cabríamos
vosotros	cabréis	vosotros	cabríais
ellos	cabrán	ellos	cabrían

IMPERFECT		*PRETERITE*	
yo	cabía	yo	cupe
tú	cabías	tú	cupiste
él	cabía	él	cupo
nosotros	cabíamos	nosotros	cupimos
vosotros	cabíais	vosotros	cupisteis
ellos	cabían	ellos	cupieron

caer *to fall*

PAST PARTICIPLE
  caído

GERUND
  cayendo

IMPERATIVE
  cae
  caed

PRESENT

yo	caigo
tú	caes
él	cae
nosotros	caemos
vosotros	caéis
ellos	caen

FUTURE

yo	caeré
tú	caerás
él	caerá
nosotros	caeremos
vosotros	caeréis
ellos	caerán

IMPERFECT

yo	caía
tú	caías
él	caía
nosotros	caíamos
vosotros	caíais
ellos	caían

PRESENT SUBJUNCTIVE

yo	caiga
tú	caigas
él	caiga
nosotros	caigamos
vosotros	caigáis
ellos	caigan

CONDITIONAL

yo	caería
tú	caerías
él	caería
nosotros	caeríamos
vosotros	caeríais
ellos	caerían

PRETERITE

yo	caí
tú	caíste
él	cayó
nosotros	caímos
vosotros	caísteis
ellos	cayeron

cocer *to boil*

PAST PARTICIPLE
cocido

GERUND
cociendo

IMPERATIVE
cuece
coced

PRESENT

yo	cuezo
tú	cueces
él	cuece
nosotros	cocemos
vosotros	cocéis
ellos	cuecen

FUTURE

yo	coceré
tú	cocerás
él	cocerá
nosotros	coceremos
vosotros	coceréis
ellos	cocerán

IMPERFECT

yo	cocía
tú	cocías
él	cocía
nosotros	cocíamos
vosotros	cocíais
ellos	cocían

PRESENT SUBJUNCTIVE

yo	cueza
tú	cuezas
él	cueza
nosotros	cozamos
vosotros	cozáis
ellos	cuezan

CONDITIONAL

yo	cocería
tú	cocerías
él	cocería
nosotros	coceríamos
vosotros	coceríais
ellos	cocerían

PRETERITE

yo	cocí
tú	cociste
él	coció
nosotros	cocimos
vosotros	cocisteis
ellos	cocieron

coger *to catch*

PAST PARTICIPLE
cogido

GERUND
cogiendo

IMPERATIVE
coge
coged

PRESENT			*PRESENT SUBJUNCTIVE*	
yo	cojo		yo	coja
tú	coges		tú	cojas
él	coge		él	coja
nosotros	cogemos		nosotros	cojamos
vosotros	cogéis		vosotros	cojáis
ellos	cogen		ellos	cojan

FUTURE			*CONDITIONAL*	
yo	cogeré		yo	cogería
tú	cogerás		tú	cogerías
él	cogerá		él	cogería
nosotros	cogeremos		nosotros	cogeríamos
vosotros	cogeréis		vosotros	cogeríais
ellos	cogerán		ellos	cogerían

IMPERFECT			*PRETERITE*	
yo	cogía		yo	cogí
tú	cogías		tú	cogiste
él	cogía		él	cogió
nosotros	cogíamos		nosotros	cogimos
vosotros	cogíais		vosotros	cogisteis
ellos	cogían		ellos	cogieron

conducir *to drive, to lead*

PAST PARTICIPLE
conducido

GERUND
conduciendo

IMPERATIVE
conduce
conducid

PRESENT

yo	conduzco
tú	conduces
él	conduce
nosotros	conducimos
vosotros	conducís
ellos	conducen

FUTURE

yo	conduciré
tú	conducirás
él	conducirá
nosotros	conduciremos
vosotros	conduciréis
ellos	conducirán

IMPERFECT

yo	conducía
tú	conducías
él	conducía
nosotros	conducíamos
vosotros	conducíais
ellos	conducían

PRESENT SUBJUNCTIVE

yo	conduzca
tú	conduzcas
él	conduzca
nosotros	conduzcamos
vosotros	conduzcáis
ellos	conduzcan

CONDITIONAL

yo	conduciría
tú	conducirías
él	conduciría
nosotros	conduciríamos
vosotros	conduciríais
ellos	conducirían

PRETERITE

yo	conduje
tú	condujiste
él	condujo
nosotros	condujimos
vosotros	condujisteis
ellos	condujeron

construir *to build*

PAST PARTICIPLE
construido

GERUND
construyendo

IMPERATIVE
construye
construid

PRESENT

yo	construyo
tú	construyes
él	construye
nosotros	construimos
vosotros	construís
ellos	construyen

FUTURE

yo	construiré
tú	construirás
él	construirá
nosotros	construiremos
vosotros	construiréis
ellos	construirán

IMPERFECT

yo	construía
tú	construías
él	construía
nosotros	construíamos
vosotros	construíais
ellos	construían

PRESENT SUBJUNCTIVE

yo	construya
tú	construyas
él	construya
nosotros	construyamos
vosotros	construyáis
ellos	construyan

CONDITIONAL

yo	construiría
tú	construirías
él	construiría
nosotros	construiríamos
vosotros	construiríais
ellos	construirían

PRETERITE

yo	construí
tú	construiste
él	construyó
nosotros	construimos
vosotros	construisteis
ellos	construyeron

contar *to tell, to count*

PAST PARTICIPLE
  contado

IMPERATIVE
  cuenta
  contad

GERUND
  contando

PRESENT

yo	cuento
tú	cuentas
él	cuenta
nosotros	contamos
vosotros	contáis
ellos	cuentan

PRESENT SUBJUNCTIVE

yo	cuente
tú	cuentes
él	cuente
nosotros	contemos
vosotros	contéis
ellos	cuenten

FUTURE

yo	contaré
tú	contarás
él	contará
nosotros	contaremos
vosotros	contaréis
ellos	contarán

CONDITIONAL

yo	contaría
tú	contarías
él	contaría
nosotros	contaríamos
vosotros	contaríais
ellos	contarían

IMPERFECT

yo	contaba
tú	contabas
él	contaba
nosotros	contábamos
vosotros	contabais
ellos	contaban

PRETERITE

yo	conté
tú	contaste
él	contó
nosotros	contamos
vosotros	contasteis
ellos	contaron

crecer *to grow*

PAST PARTICIPLE
  crecido

GERUND
  creciendo

IMPERATIVE
  crece
  creced

PRESENT
yo	crezco
tú	creces
él	crece
nosotros	crecemos
vosotros	crecéis
ellos	crecen

FUTURE
yo	creceré
tú	crecerás
él	crecerá
nosotros	creceremos
vosotros	creceréis
ellos	crecerán

IMPERFECT
yo	crecía
tú	crecías
él	crecía
nosotros	crecíamos
vosotros	crecíais
ellos	crecían

PRESENT SUBJUNCTIVE
yo	crezca
tú	crezcas
él	crezca
nosotros	crezcamos
vosotros	crezcáis
ellos	crezcan

CONDITIONAL
yo	crecería
tú	crecerías
él	crecería
nosotros	creceríamos
vosotros	creceríais
ellos	crecerían

PRETERITE
yo	crecí
tú	creciste
él	creció
nosotros	crecimos
vosotros	crecisteis
ellos	crecieron

cruzar *to cross*

PAST PARTICIPLE	IMPERATIVE
cruzado	cruza
	cruzad

GERUND
cruzando

PRESENT		PRESENT SUBJUNCTIVE	
yo	cruzo	yo	cruce
tú	cruzas	tú	cruces
él	cruza	él	cruce
nosotros	cruzamos	nosotros	crucemos
vosotros	cruzáis	vosotros	crucéis
ellos	cruzan	ellos	crucen

FUTURE		CONDITIONAL	
yo	cruzaré	yo	cruzaría
tú	cruzarás	tú	cruzarías
él	cruzará	él	cruzaría
nosotros	cruzaremos	nosotros	cruzaríamos
vosotros	cruzaréis	vosotros	cruzaríais
ellos	cruzarán	ellos	cruzarían

IMPERFECT		PRETERITE	
yo	cruzaba	yo	crucé
tú	cruzabas	tú	cruzaste
él	cruzaba	él	cruzó
nosotros	cruzábamos	nosotros	cruzamos
vosotros	cruzabais	vosotros	cruzasteis
ellos	cruzaban	ellos	cruzaron

cubrir *to cover*

PAST PARTICIPLE
cubierto

GERUND
cubriendo

IMPERATIVE
cubre
cubrid

PRESENT			*PRESENT SUBJUNCTIVE*	
yo	cubro		yo	cubra
tú	cubres		tú	cubras
él	cubre		él	cubra
nosotros	cubrimos		nosotros	cubramos
vosotros	cubrís		vosotros	cubráis
ellos	cubren		ellos	cubran

FUTURE			*CONDITIONAL*	
yo	cubriré		yo	cubriría
tú	cubrirás		tú	cubrirías
él	cubrirá		él	cubriría
nosotros	cubriremos		nosotros	cubriríamos
vosotros	cubriréis		vosotros	cubriríais
ellos	cubrirán		ellos	cubrirían

IMPERFECT			*PRETERITE*	
yo	cubría		yo	cubrí
tú	cubrías		tú	cubriste
él	cubría		él	cubrió
nosotros	cubríamos		nosotros	cubrimos
vosotros	cubríais		vosotros	cubristeis
ellos	cubrían		ellos	cubrieron

dar to give

PAST PARTICIPLE	IMPERATIVE
dado	da
	dad

GERUND
dando

PRESENT		PRESENT SUBJUNCTIVE	
yo	doy	yo	dé
tú	das	tú	des
él	da	él	dé
nosotros	damos	nosotros	demos
vosotros	dais	vosotros	deis
ellos	dan	ellos	den

FUTURE		CONDITIONAL	
yo	daré	yo	daría
tú	darás	tú	darías
él	dará	él	daría
nosotros	daremos	nosotros	daríamos
vosotros	daréis	vosotros	daríais
ellos	darán	ellos	darían

IMPERFECT		PRETERITE	
yo	daba	yo	di
tú	dabas	tú	diste
él	daba	él	dio
nosotros	dábamos	nosotros	dimos
vosotros	dabais	vosotros	disteis
ellos	daban	ellos	dieron

decir *to say*

PAST PARTICIPLE
dicho

GERUND
diciendo

IMPERATIVE
di
decid

PRESENT
yo	digo
tú	dices
él	dice
nosotros	decimos
vosotros	decís
ellos	dicen

FUTURE
yo	diré
tú	dirás
él	dirá
nosotros	diremos
vosotros	diréis
ellos	dirán

IMPERFECT
yo	decía
tú	decías
él	decía
nosotros	decíamos
vosotros	decíais
ellos	decían

PRESENT SUBJUNCTIVE
yo	diga
tú	digas
él	diga
nosotros	digamos
vosotros	digáis
ellos	digan

CONDITIONAL
yo	diría
tú	dirías
él	diría
nosotros	diríamos
vosotros	diríais
ellos	dirían

PRETERITE
yo	dije
tú	dijiste
él	dijo
nosotros	dijimos
vosotros	dijisteis
ellos	dijeron

dirigir *to direct*

PAST PARTICIPLE
dirigido

GERUND
dirigiendo

IMPERATIVE
dirige
dirigid

PRESENT

yo	dirijo
tú	diriges
él	dirige
nosotros	dirigimos
vosotros	dirigís
ellos	dirigen

FUTURE

yo	dirigiré
tú	dirigirás
él	dirigirá
nosotros	dirigiremos
vosotros	dirigiréis
ellos	dirigirán

IMPERFECT

yo	dirigía
tú	dirigías
él	dirigía
nosotros	dirigíamos
vosotros	dirigíais
ellos	dirigían

PRESENT SUBJUNCTIVE

yo	dirija
tú	dirijas
él	dirija
nosotros	dirijamos
vosotros	dirijáis
ellos	dirijan

CONDITIONAL

yo	dirigiría
tú	dirigirías
él	dirigiría
nosotros	dirigiríamos
vosotros	dirigiríais
ellos	dirigirían

PRETERITE

yo	dirigí
tú	dirigiste
él	dirigió
nosotros	dirigimos
vosotros	dirigisteis
ellos	dirigieron

distinguir *to distinguish*

PAST PARTICIPLE
distinguido

IMPERATIVE
distingue
distinguid

GERUND
distinguiendo

PRESENT

yo	distingo
tú	distingues
él	distingue
nosotros	distinguimos
vosotros	distinguís
ellos	distinguen

PRESENT SUBJUNCTIVE

yo	distinga
tú	distingas
él	distinga
nosotros	distingamos
vosotros	distingáis
ellos	distingan

FUTURE

yo	distinguiré
tú	distinguirás
él	distinguirá
nosotros	distinguiremos
vosotros	distinguiréis
ellos	distinguirán

CONDITIONAL

yo	distinguiría
tú	distinguirías
él	distinguiría
nosotros	distinguiríamos
vosotros	distinguiríais
ellos	distinguirían

IMPERFECT

yo	distinguía
tú	distinguías
él	distinguía
nosotros	distinguíamos
vosotros	distinguíais
ellos	distinguían

PRETERITE

yo	distinguí
tú	distinguiste
él	distinguió
nosotros	distinguimos
vosotros	distinguisteis
ellos	distinguieron

dormir *to sleep*

PAST PARTICIPLE
dormido

IMPERATIVE
duerme
dormid

GERUND
durmiendo

PRESENT			*PRESENT SUBJUNCTIVE*	
yo	duermo		yo	duerma
tú	duermes		tú	duermas
él	duerme		él	duerma
nosotros	dormimos		nosotros	durmamos
vosotros	dormís		vosotros	durmáis
ellos	duermen		ellos	duerman
FUTURE			*CONDITIONAL*	
yo	dormiré		yo	dormiría
tú	dormirás		tú	dormirías
él	dormirá		él	dormiría
nosotros	dormiremos		nosotros	dormiríamos
vosotros	dormiréis		vosotros	dormiríais
ellos	dormirán		ellos	dormirían
IMPERFECT			*PRETERITE*	
yo	dormía		yo	dormí
tú	dormías		tú	dormiste
él	dormía		él	durmió
nosotros	dormíamos		nosotros	dormimos
vosotros	dormíais		vosotros	dormisteis
ellos	dormían		ellos	durmieron

elegir *to choose*

PAST PARTICIPLE
elegido

GERUND
eligiendo

IMPERATIVE
elige
elegid

PRESENT		*PRESENT SUBJUNCTIVE*	
yo	elijo	yo	elija
tú	eliges	tú	elijas
él	elige	él	elija
nosotros	elegimos	nosotros	elijamos
vosotros	elegís	vosotros	elijáis
ellos	eligen	ellos	elijan

FUTURE		*CONDITIONAL*	
yo	elegiré	yo	elegiría
tú	elegirás	tú	elegirías
él	elegirá	él	elegiría
nosotros	elegiremos	nosotros	elegiríamos
vosotros	elegiréis	vosotros	elegiríais
ellos	elegirán	ellos	elegirían

IMPERFECT		*PRETERITE*	
yo	elegía	yo	elegí
tú	elegías	tú	elegiste
él	elegía	él	eligió
nosotros	elegíamos	nosotros	elegimos
vosotros	elegíais	vosotros	elegisteis
ellos	elegían	ellos	eligieron

empezar *to begin*

PAST PARTICIPLE
empezado

GERUND
empezando

IMPERATIVE
empieza
empezad

PRESENT

yo	empiezo
tú	empiezas
él	empieza
nosotros	empezamos
vosotros	empezáis
ellos	empiezan

FUTURE

yo	empezaré
tú	empezarás
él	empezará
nosotros	empezaremos
vosotros	empezaréis
ellos	empezarán

IMPERFECT

yo	empezaba
tú	empezabas
él	empezaba
nosotros	empezábamos
vosotros	empezabais
ellos	empezaban

PRESENT SUBJUNCTIVE

yo	empiece
tú	empieces
él	empiece
nosotros	empecemos
vosotros	empecéis
ellos	empiecen

CONDITIONAL

yo	empezaría
tú	empezarías
él	empezaría
nosotros	empezaríamos
vosotros	empezaríais
ellos	empezarían

PRETERITE

yo	empecé
tú	empezaste
él	empezó
nosotros	empezamos
vosotros	empezasteis
ellos	empezaron

entender *to understand*

PAST PARTICIPLE
entendido

IMPERATIVE
entiende
entended

GERUND
entendiendo

PRESENT

yo	entiendo
tú	entiendes
él	entiende
nosotros	entendemos
vosotros	entendéis
ellos	entienden

PRESENT SUBJUNCTIVE

yo	entienda
tú	entiendas
él	entienda
nosotros	entendamos
vosotros	entendáis
ellos	entiendan

FUTURE

yo	entenderé
tú	entenderás
él	entenderá
nosotros	entenderemos
vosotros	entenderéis
ellos	entenderán

CONDITIONAL

yo	entendería
tú	entenderías
él	entendería
nosotros	entenderíamos
vosotros	entenderíais
ellos	entenderían

IMPERFECT

yo	entendía
tú	entendías
él	entendía
nosotros	entendíamos
vosotros	entendíais
ellos	entendían

PRETERITE

yo	entendí
tú	entendiste
él	entendió
nosotros	entendimos
vosotros	entendisteis
ellos	entendieron

enviar *to send*

PAST PARTICIPLE
enviado

IMPERATIVE
envía
enviad

GERUND
enviando

PRESENT		*PRESENT SUBJUNCTIVE*	
yo	envío	yo	envíe
tú	envías	tú	envíes
él	envía	él	envíe
nosotros	enviamos	nosotros	enviemos
vosotros	enviáis	vosotros	enviéis
ellos	envían	ellos	envíen

FUTURE		*CONDITIONAL*	
yo	enviaré	yo	enviaría
tú	enviarás	tú	enviarías
él	enviará	él	enviaría
nosotros	enviaremos	nosotros	enviaríamos
vosotros	enviaréis	vosotros	enviaríais
ellos	enviarán	ellos	enviarían

IMPERFECT		*PRETERITE*	
yo	enviaba	yo	envié
tú	enviabas	tú	enviaste
él	enviaba	él	envió
nosotros	enviábamos	nosotros	enviamos
vosotros	enviabais	vosotros	enviasteis
ellos	enviaban	ellos	enviaron

erguir *to erect*

PAST PARTICIPLE
erguido

IMPERATIVE
yergue
erguid

GERUND
irguiendo

PRESENT		*PRESENT SUBJUNCTIVE*	
yo	yergo	yo	yerga
tú	yergues	tú	yergas
él	yergue	él	yerga
nosotros	erguimos	nosotros	irgamos
vosotros	erguís	vosotros	irgáis
ellos	yerguen	ellos	yergan

FUTURE		*CONDITIONAL*	
yo	erguiré	yo	erguiría
tú	erguirás	tú	erguirías
él	erguirá	él	erguiría
nosotros	erguiremos	nosotros	erguiríamos
vosotros	erguiréis	vosotros	erguiríais
ellos	erguirán	ellos	erguirían

IMPERFECT		*PRETERITE*	
yo	erguía	yo	erguí
tú	erguías	tú	erguiste
él	erguía	él	irguió
nosotros	erguíamos	nosotros	erguimos
vosotros	erguíais	vosotros	erguisteis
ellos	erguían	ellos	irguieron

errar *to err*

PAST PARTICIPLE
errado

IMPERATIVE
yerra
errad

GERUND
errando

PRESENT		PRESENT SUBJUNCTIVE	
yo	yerro	yo	yerre
tú	yerras	tú	yerres
él	yerra	él	yerre
nosotros	erramos	nosotros	erremos
vosotros	erráis	vosotros	erréis
ellos	yerran	ellos	yerren

FUTURE		CONDITIONAL	
yo	erraré	yo	erraría
tú	errarás	tú	errarías
él	errará	él	erraría
nosotros	erraremos	nosotros	erraríamos
vosotros	erraréis	vosotros	erraríais
ellos	errarán	ellos	errarían

IMPERFECT		PRETERITE	
yo	erraba	yo	erré
tú	errabas	tú	erraste
él	erraba	él	erró
nosotros	errábamos	nosotros	erramos
vosotros	errabais	vosotros	errasteis
ellos	erraban	ellos	erraron

escribir *to write*

PAST PARTICIPLE
escrito

GERUND
escribiendo

IMPERATIVE
escribe
escribid

PRESENT		PRESENT SUBJUNCTIVE	
yo	escribo	yo	escriba
tú	escribes	tú	escribas
él	escribe	él	escriba
nosotros	escribimos	nosotros	escribamos
vosotros	escribís	vosotros	escribáis
ellos	escriben	ellos	escriban

FUTURE		CONDITIONAL	
yo	escribiré	yo	escribiría
tú	escribirás	tú	escribirías
él	escribirá	él	escribiría
nosotros	escribiremos	nosotros	escribiríamos
vosotros	escribiréis	vosotros	escribiríais
ellos	escribirán	ellos	escribirían

IMPERFECT		PRETERITE	
yo	escribía	yo	escribí
tú	escribías	tú	escribiste
él	escribía	él	escribió
nosotros	escribíamos	nosotros	escribimos
vosotros	escribíais	vosotros	escribisteis
ellos	escribían	ellos	escribieron

estar *to be*

PAST PARTICIPLE
  estado

IMPERATIVE
  está
  estad

GERUND
  estando

PRESENT

yo	estoy
tú	estás
él	está
nosotros	estamos
vosotros	estáis
ellos	están

PRESENT SUBJUNCTIVE

yo	esté
tú	estés
él	esté
nosotros	estemos
vosotros	estéis
ellos	estén

FUTURE

yo	estaré
tú	estarás
él	estará
nosotros	estaremos
vosotros	estaréis
ellos	estarán

CONDITIONAL

yo	estaría
tú	estarías
él	estaría
nosotros	estaríamos
vosotros	estaríais
ellos	estarían

IMPERFECT

yo	estaba
tú	estabas
él	estaba
nosotros	estábamos
vosotros	estabais
ellos	estaban

PRETERITE

yo	estuve
tú	estuviste
él	estuvo
nosotros	estuvimos
vosotros	estuvisteis
ellos	estuvieron

freír *to fry*

PAST PARTICIPLE
  frito

IMPERATIVE
  fríe
  freíd

GERUND
  friendo

PRESENT		PRESENT SUBJUNCTIVE	
yo	frío	yo	fría
tú	fríes	tú	frías
él	fríe	él	fría
nosotros	freímos	nosotros	friamos
vosotros	freís	vosotros	friáis
ellos	fríen	ellos	frían

FUTURE		CONDITIONAL	
yo	freiré	yo	freiría
tú	freirás	tú	freirías
él	freirá	él	freiría
nosotros	freiremos	nosotros	freiríamos
vosotros	freiréis	vosotros	freiríais
ellos	freirán	ellos	freirían

IMPERFECT		PRETERITE	
yo	freía	yo	freí
tú	freías	tú	freíste
él	freía	él	frió
nosotros	freíamos	nosotros	freímos
vosotros	freíais	vosotros	freísteis
ellos	freían	ellos	frieron

gruñir *to grunt*

PAST PARTICIPLE
  gruñido

GERUND
  gruñendo

IMPERATIVE
  gruñe
  gruñid

PRESENT		PRESENT SUBJUNCTIVE	
yo	gruño	yo	gruña
tú	gruñes	tú	gruñas
él	gruñe	él	gruña
nosotros	gruñimos	nosotros	gruñamos
vosotros	gruñís	vosotros	gruñáis
ellos	gruñen	ellos	gruñan

FUTURE		CONDITIONAL	
yo	gruñiré	yo	gruñiría
tú	gruñirás	tú	gruñirías
él	gruñirá	él	gruñiría
nosotros	gruñiremos	nosotros	gruñiríamos
vosotros	gruñiréis	vosotros	gruñiríais
ellos	gruñirán	ellos	gruñirían

IMPERFECT		PRETERITE	
yo	gruñía	yo	gruñí
tú	gruñías	tú	gruñiste
él	gruñía	él	gruñó
nosotros	gruñíamos	nosotros	gruñimos
vosotros	gruñíais	vosotros	gruñisteis
ellos	gruñían	ellos	gruñeron

haber *to have (auxiliary)*

PAST PARTICIPLE
habido

IMPERATIVE
not used

GERUND
habiendo

PRESENT

yo	he
tú	has
él	ha
nosotros	hemos
vosotros	habéis
ellos	han

PRESENT SUBJUNCTIVE

yo	haya
tú	hayas
él	haya
nosotros	hayamos
vosotros	hayáis
ellos	hayan

FUTURE

yo	habré
tú	habrás
él	habrá
nosotros	habremos
vosotros	habréis
ellos	habrán

CONDITIONAL

yo	habría
tú	habrías
él	habría
nosotros	habríamos
vosotros	habríais
ellos	habrían

IMPERFECT

yo	había
tú	habías
él	había
nosotros	habíamos
vosotros	habíais
ellos	habían

PRETERITE

yo	hube
tú	hubiste
él	hubo
nosotros	hubimos
vosotros	hubisteis
ellos	hubieron

hacer *to do, to make*

PAST PARTICIPLE
  hecho

IMPERATIVE
  haz
  haced

GERUND
  haciendo

PRESENT	
yo	hago
tú	haces
él	hace
nosotros	hacemos
vosotros	hacéis
ellos	hacen

PRESENT SUBJUNCTIVE	
yo	haga
tú	hagas
él	haga
nosotros	hagamos
vosotros	hagáis
ellos	hagan

FUTURE	
yo	haré
tú	harás
él	hará
nosotros	haremos
vosotros	haréis
ellos	harán

CONDITIONAL	
yo	haría
tú	harías
él	haría
nosotros	haríamos
vosotros	haríais
ellos	harían

IMPERFECT	
yo	hacía
tú	hacías
él	hacía
nosotros	hacíamos
vosotros	hacíais
ellos	hacían

PRETERITE	
yo	hice
tú	hiciste
él	hizo
nosotros	hicimos
vosotros	hicisteis
ellos	hicieron

hay *there is, there are*

PAST PARTICIPLE
hab**ido**

IMPERATIVE
not used

GERUND
hab**iendo**

PRESENT
        hay

PRESENT SUBJUNCTIVE
        haya

FUTURE
        habrá

CONDITIONAL
        habría

IMPERFECT
        hab**ía**

PRETERITE
        hubo

ir *to go*

PAST PARTICIPLE	IMPERATIVE
ido	ve
	id

GERUND
  yendo

PRESENT

yo	voy
tú	vas
él	va
nosotros	vamos
vosotros	vais
ellos	van

PRESENT SUBJUNCTIVE

yo	vaya
tú	vayas
él	vaya
nosotros	vayamos
vosotros	vayáis
ellos	vayan

FUTURE

yo	iré
tú	irás
él	irá
nosotros	iremos
vosotros	iréis
ellos	irán

CONDITIONAL

yo	iría
tú	irías
él	iría
nosotros	iríamos
vosotros	iríais
ellos	irían

IMPERFECT

yo	iba
tú	ibas
él	iba
nosotros	íbamos
vosotros	ibais
ellos	iban

PRETERITE

yo	fui
tú	fuiste
él	fue
nosotros	fuimos
vosotros	fuisteis
ellos	fueron

jugar *to play*

PAST PARTICIPLE
jugado

GERUND
jugando

IMPERATIVE
juega
jugad

PRESENT		*PRESENT SUBJUNCTIVE*	
yo	juego	yo	juegue
tú	juegas	tú	juegues
él	juega	él	juegue
nosotros	jugamos	nosotros	juguemos
vosotros	jugáis	vosotros	juguéis
ellos	juegan	ellos	jueguen

FUTURE		*CONDITIONAL*	
yo	jugaré	yo	jugaría
tú	jugarás	tú	jugarías
él	jugará	él	jugaría
nosotros	jugaremos	nosotros	jugaríamos
vosotros	jugaréis	vosotros	jugaríais
ellos	jugarán	ellos	jugarían

IMPERFECT		*PRETERITE*	
yo	jugaba	yo	jugué
tú	jugabas	tú	jugaste
él	jugaba	él	jugó
nosotros	jugábamos	nosotros	jugamos
vosotros	jugabais	vosotros	jugasteis
ellos	jugaban	ellos	jugaron

leer *to read*

PAST PARTICIPLE
leído

GERUND
leyendo

IMPERATIVE
lee
leed

PRESENT

yo	leo
tú	lees
él	lee
nosotros	leemos
vosotros	leéis
ellos	leen

FUTURE

yo	leeré
tú	leerás
él	leerá
nosotros	leeremos
vosotros	leeréis
ellos	leerán

IMPERFECT

yo	leía
tú	leías
él	leía
nosotros	leíamos
vosotros	leíais
ellos	leían

PRESENT SUBJUNCTIVE

yo	lea
tú	leas
él	lea
nosotros	leamos
vosotros	leáis
ellos	lean

CONDITIONAL

yo	leería
tú	leerías
él	leería
nosotros	leeríamos
vosotros	leeríais
ellos	leerían

PRETERITE

yo	leí
tú	leíste
él	leyó
nosotros	leímos
vosotros	leísteis
ellos	leyeron

lucir *to shine*

PAST PARTICIPLE
lucido

GERUND
luciendo

IMPERATIVE
luce
lucid

PRESENT		*PRESENT SUBJUNCTIVE*	
yo	luzco	yo	luzca
tú	luces	tú	luzcas
él	luce	él	luzca
nosotros	lucimos	nosotros	luzcamos
vosotros	lucís	vosotros	luzcáis
ellos	lucen	ellos	luzcan
FUTURE		*CONDITIONAL*	
yo	luciré	yo	luciría
tú	lucirás	tú	lucirías
él	lucirá	él	luciría
nosotros	luciremos	nosotros	luciríamos
vosotros	luciréis	vosotros	luciríais
ellos	lucirán	ellos	lucirían
IMPERFECT		*PRETERITE*	
yo	lucía	yo	lucí
tú	lucías	tú	luciste
él	lucía	él	lució
nosotros	lucíamos	nosotros	lucimos
vosotros	lucíais	vosotros	lucisteis
ellos	lucían	ellos	lucieron

llover *to rain*

PAST PARTICIPLE
llovido

IMPERATIVE
not used

GERUND
lloviendo

PRESENT
llueve

PRESENT SUBJUNCTIVE
llueva

FUTURE
lloverá

CONDITIONAL
llovería

IMPERFECT
llovía

PRETERITE
llovió

morir *to die*

PAST PARTICIPLE
muerto

IMPERATIVE
muere
morid

GERUND
muriendo

PRESENT

yo	muero
tú	mueres
él	muere
nosotros	morimos
vosotros	morís
ellos	mueren

FUTURE

yo	moriré
tú	morirás
él	morirá
nosotros	moriremos
vosotros	moriréis
ellos	morirán

IMPERFECT

yo	moría
tú	morías
él	moría
nosotros	moríamos
vosotros	moríais
ellos	morían

PRESENT SUBJUNCTIVE

yo	muera
tú	mueras
él	muera
nosotros	muramos
vosotros	muráis
ellos	mueran

CONDITIONAL

yo	moriría
tú	morirías
él	moriría
nosotros	moriríamos
vosotros	moriríais
ellos	morirían

PRETERITE

yo	morí
tú	moriste
él	murió
nosotros	morimos
vosotros	moristeis
ellos	murieron

mover *to move*

PAST PARTICIPLE
movido

IMPERATIVE
mueve
moved

GERUND
moviendo

PRESENT		PRESENT SUBJUNCTIVE	
yo	muevo	yo	mueva
tú	mueves	tú	muevas
él	mueve	él	mueva
nosotros	movemos	nosotros	movamos
vosotros	movéis	vosotros	mováis
ellos	mueven	ellos	muevan

FUTURE		CONDITIONAL	
yo	moveré	yo	movería
tú	moverás	tú	moverías
él	moverá	él	movería
nosotros	moveremos	nosotros	moveríamos
vosotros	moveréis	vosotros	moveríais
ellos	moverán	ellos	moverían

IMPERFECT		PRETERITE	
yo	movía	yo	moví
tú	movías	tú	moviste
él	movía	él	movió
nosotros	movíamos	nosotros	movimos
vosotros	movíais	vosotros	movisteis
ellos	movían	ellos	movieron

nacer *to be born*

PAST PARTICIPLE
nacido

IMPERATIVE
nace
naced

GERUND
naciendo

PRESENT		PRESENT SUBJUNCTIVE	
yo	nazco	yo	nazca
tú	naces	tú	nazcas
él	nace	él	nazca
nosotros	nacemos	nosotros	nazcamos
vosotros	nacéis	vosotros	nazcáis
ellos	nacen	ellos	nazcan

FUTURE		CONDITIONAL	
yo	naceré	yo	nacería
tú	nacerás	tú	nacerías
él	nacerá	él	nacería
nosotros	naceremos	nosotros	naceríamos
vosotros	naceréis	vosotros	naceríais
ellos	nacerán	ellos	nacerían

IMPERFECT		PRETERITE	
yo	nacía	yo	nací
tú	nacías	tú	naciste
él	nacía	él	nació
nosotros	nacíamos	nosotros	nacimos
vosotros	nacíais	vosotros	nacisteis
ellos	nacían	ellos	nacieron

negar *to deny*

PAST PARTICIPLE
negado

GERUND
negando

IMPERATIVE
niega
negad

PRESENT
yo	niego
tú	niegas
él	niega
nosotros	negamos
vosotros	negáis
ellos	niegan

FUTURE
yo	negaré
tú	negarás
él	negará
nosotros	negaremos
vosotros	negaréis
ellos	negarán

IMPERFECT
yo	negaba
tú	negabas
él	negaba
nosotros	negábamos
vosotros	negabais
ellos	negaban

PRESENT SUBJUNCTIVE
yo	niegue
tú	niegues
él	niegue
nosotros	neguemos
vosotros	neguéis
ellos	nieguen

CONDITIONAL
yo	negaría
tú	negarías
él	negaría
nosotros	negaríamos
vosotros	negaríais
ellos	negarían

PRETERITE
yo	negué
tú	negaste
él	negó
nosotros	negamos
vosotros	negasteis
ellos	negaron

oír *to hear*

PAST PARTICIPLE
oído

IMPERATIVE
oye
oíd

GERUND
oyendo

PRESENT
yo	oigo
tú	oyes
él	oye
nosotros	oímos
vosotros	oís
ellos	oyen

PRESENT SUBJUNCTIVE
yo	oiga
tú	oigas
él	oiga
nosotros	oigamos
vosotros	oigáis
ellos	oigan

FUTURE
yo	oiré
tú	oirás
él	oirá
nosotros	oiremos
vosotros	oiréis
ellos	oirán

CONDITIONAL
yo	oiría
tú	oirías
él	oiría
nosotros	oiríamos
vosotros	oiríais
ellos	oirían

IMPERFECT
yo	oía
tú	oías
él	oía
nosotros	oíamos
vosotros	oíais
ellos	oían

PRETERITE
yo	oí
tú	oíste
él	oyó
nosotros	oímos
vosotros	oísteis
ellos	oyeron

oler *to smell*

PAST PARTICIPLE
olido

IMPERATIVE
huele
oled

GERUND
oliendo

PRESENT

yo	huelo
tú	hueles
él	huele
nosotros	olemos
vosotros	oléis
ellos	huelen

PRESENT SUBJUNCTIVE

yo	huela
tú	huelas
él	huela
nosotros	olamos
vosotros	oláis
ellos	huelan

FUTURE

yo	oleré
tú	olerás
él	olerá
nosotros	oleremos
vosotros	oleréis
ellos	olerán

CONDITIONAL

yo	olería
tú	olerías
él	olería
nosotros	oleríamos
vosotros	oleríais
ellos	olerían

IMPERFECT

yo	olía
tú	olías
él	olía
nosotros	olíamos
vosotros	olíais
ellos	olían

PRETERITE

yo	olí
tú	oliste
él	olió
nosotros	olimos
vosotros	olisteis
ellos	olieron

pagar *to pay*

PAST PARTICIPLE
  pagado

GERUND
  pagando

IMPERATIVE
  paga
  pagad

PRESENT

yo	pago
tú	pagas
él	paga
nosotros	pagamos
vosotros	pagáis
ellos	pagan

FUTURE

yo	pagaré
tú	pagarás
él	pagará
nosotros	pagaremos
vosotros	pagaréis
ellos	pagarán

IMPERFECT

yo	pagaba
tú	pagabas
él	pagaba
nosotros	pagábamos
vosotros	pagabais
ellos	pagaban

PRESENT SUBJUNCTIVE

yo	pague
tú	pagues
él	pague
nosotros	paguemos
vosotros	paguéis
ellos	paguen

CONDITIONAL

yo	pagaría
tú	pagarías
él	pagaría
nosotros	pagaríamos
vosotros	pagaríais
ellos	pagarían

PRETERITE

yo	pagué
tú	pagaste
él	pagó
nosotros	pagamos
vosotros	pagasteis
ellos	pagaron

pedir *to ask for*

PAST PARTICIPLE
 pedido

IMPERATIVE
 pide
 pedid

GERUND
 pidiendo

PRESENT

yo	pido
tú	pides
él	pide
nosotros	pedimos
vosotros	pedís
ellos	piden

PRESENT SUBJUNCTIVE

yo	pida
tú	pidas
él	pida
nosotros	pidamos
vosotros	pidáis
ellos	pidan

FUTURE

yo	pediré
tú	pedirás
él	pedirá
nosotros	pediremos
vosotros	pediréis
ellos	pedirán

CONDITIONAL

yo	pediría
tú	pedirías
él	pediría
nosotros	pediríamos
vosotros	pediríais
ellos	pedirían

IMPERFECT

yo	pedía
tú	pedías
él	pedía
nosotros	pedíamos
vosotros	pedíais
ellos	pedían

PRETERITE

yo	pedí
tú	pediste
él	pidió
nosotros	pedimos
vosotros	pedisteis
ellos	pidieron

pensar *to think*

PAST PARTICIPLE
pensado

GERUND
pensando

IMPERATIVE
piensa
pensad

PRESENT
yo	pienso
tú	piensas
él	piensa
nosotros	pensamos
vosotros	pensáis
ellos	piensan

PRESENT SUBJUNCTIVE
yo	piense
tú	pienses
él	piense
nosotros	pensemos
vosotros	penséis
ellos	piensen

FUTURE
yo	pensaré
tú	pensarás
él	pensará
nosotros	pensaremos
vosotros	pensaréis
ellos	pensarán

CONDITIONAL
yo	pensaría
tú	pensarías
él	pensaría
nosotros	pensaríamos
vosotros	pensaríais
ellos	pensarían

IMPERFECT
yo	pensaba
tú	pensabas
él	pensaba
nosotros	pensábamos
vosotros	pensabais
ellos	pensaban

PRETERITE
yo	pensé
tú	pensaste
él	pensó
nosotros	pensamos
vosotros	pensasteis
ellos	pensaron

poder *to be able*

PAST PARTICIPLE
  podido

GERUND
  pudiendo

IMPERATIVE
  puede
  poded

PRESENT		*PRESENT SUBJUNCTIVE*	
yo	puedo	yo	pueda
tú	puedes	tú	puedas
él	puede	él	pueda
nosotros	podemos	nosotros	podamos
vosotros	podéis	vosotros	podáis
ellos	pueden	ellos	puedan

FUTURE		*CONDITIONAL*	
yo	podré	yo	podría
tú	podrás	tú	podrías
él	podrá	él	podría
nosotros	podremos	nosotros	podríamos
vosotros	podréis	vosotros	podríais
ellos	podrán	ellos	podrían

IMPERFECT		*PRETERITE*	
yo	podía	yo	pude
tú	podías	tú	pudiste
él	podía	él	pudo
nosotros	podíamos	nosotros	pudimos
vosotros	podíais	vosotros	pudisteis
ellos	podían	ellos	pudieron

poner *to put*

PAST PARTICIPLE
puesto

GERUND
poniendo

IMPERATIVE
pon
poned

PRESENT		PRESENT SUBJUNCTIVE	
yo	pongo	yo	ponga
tú	pones	tú	pongas
él	pone	él	ponga
nosotros	ponemos	nosotros	pongamos
vosotros	ponéis	vosotros	pongáis
ellos	ponen	ellos	pongan

FUTURE		CONDITIONAL	
yo	pondré	yo	pondría
tú	pondrás	tú	pondrías
él	pondrá	él	pondría
nosotros	pondremos	nosotros	pondríamos
vosotros	pondréis	vosotros	pondríais
ellos	pondrán	ellos	pondrían

IMPERFECT		PRETERITE	
yo	ponía	yo	puse
tú	ponías	tú	pusiste
él	ponía	él	puso
nosotros	poníamos	nosotros	pusimos
vosotros	poníais	vosotros	pusisteis
ellos	ponían	ellos	pusieron

prohibir *to forbid*

PAST PARTICIPLE
prohibido

IMPERATIVE
prohíbe
prohibid

GERUND
prohibiendo

PRESENT
yo	prohíbo
tú	prohíbes
él	prohíbe
nosotros	prohibimos
vosotros	prohibís
ellos	prohíben

PRESENT SUBJUNCTIVE
yo	prohíba
tú	prohíbas
él	prohíba
nosotros	prohibamos
vosotros	prohibáis
ellos	prohíban

FUTURE
yo	prohibiré
tú	prohibirás
él	prohibirá
nosotros	prohibiremos
vosotros	prohibiréis
ellos	prohibirán

CONDITIONAL
yo	prohibiría
tú	prohibirías
él	prohibiría
nosotros	prohibiríamos
vosotros	probibiríais
ellos	prohibirían

IMPERFECT
yo	prohibía
tú	prohibías
él	prohibía
nosotros	prohibíamos
vosotros	prohibíais
ellos	prohibían

PRETERITE
yo	prohibí
tú	prohibiste
él	prohibió
nosotros	prohibimos
vosotros	prohibisteis
ellos	prohibieron

querer *to want*

PAST PARTICIPLE
  querido

GERUND
  queriendo

IMPERATIVE
  quiere
  quered

PRESENT		*PRESENT SUBJUNCTIVE*	
yo	quiero	yo	quiera
tú	quieres	tú	quieras
él	quiere	él	quiera
nosotros	queremos	nosotros	queramos
vosotros	queréis	vosotros	queráis
ellos	quieren	ellos	quieran

FUTURE		*CONDITIONAL*	
yo	querré	yo	querría
tú	querrás	tú	querrías
él	querrá	él	querría
nosotros	querremos	nosotros	querríamos
vosotros	querréis	vosotros	querríais
ellos	querrán	ellos	querrían

IMPERFECT		*PRETERITE*	
yo	quería	yo	quise
tú	querías	tú	quisiste
él	quería	él	quiso
nosotros	queríamos	nosotros	quisimos
vosotros	queríais	vosotros	quisisteis
ellos	querían	ellos	quisieron

rehusar *to refuse*

PAST PARTICIPLE
rehusado

IMPERATIVE
rehúsa
rehusad

GERUND
rehusando

PRESENT
yo	rehúso
tú	rehúsas
él	rehúsa
nosotros	rehusamos
vosotros	rehusáis
ellos	rehúsan

PRESENT SUBJUNCTIVE
yo	rehúse
tú	rehúses
él	rehúse
nosotros	rehusemos
vosotros	rehuséis
ellos	rehúsen

FUTURE
yo	rehusaré
tú	rehusarás
él	rehusará
nosotros	rehusaremos
vosotros	rehusaréis
ellos	rehusarán

CONDITIONAL
yo	rehusaría
tú	rehusarías
él	rehusaría
nosotros	rehusaríamos
vosotros	rehusaríais
ellos	rehusarían

IMPERFECT
yo	rehusaba
tú	rehusabas
él	rehusaba
nosotros	rehusábamos
vosotros	rehusabais
ellos	rehusaban

PRETERITE
yo	rehusé
tú	rehusaste
él	rehusó
nosotros	rehusamos
vosotros	rehusasteis
ellos	rehusaron

reír *to laugh*

PAST PARTICIPLE
reído

IMPERATIVE
ríe
reíd

GERUND
riendo

PRESENT		PRESENT SUBJUNCTIVE	
yo	río	yo	ría
tú	ríes	tú	rías
él	ríe	él	ría
nosotros	reímos	nosotros	riamos
vosotros	reís	vosotros	riáis
ellos	ríen	ellos	rían

FUTURE		CONDITIONAL	
yo	reiré	yo	reiría
tú	reirás	tú	reirías
él	reirá	él	reiría
nosotros	reiremos	nosotros	reiríamos
vosotros	reiréis	vosotros	reiríais
ellos	reirán	ellos	reirían

IMPERFECT		PRETERITE	
yo	reía	yo	reí
tú	reías	tú	reíste
él	reía	él	rió
nosotros	reíamos	nosotros	reímos
vosotros	reíais	vosotros	reísteis
ellos	reían	ellos	rieron

reñir *to scold*

PAST PARTICIPLE
reñido

IMPERATIVE
riñe
reñid

GERUND
riñendo

PRESENT

yo	riño
tú	riñes
él	riñe
nosotros	reñimos
vosotros	reñís
ellos	riñen

PRESENT SUBJUNCTIVE

yo	riña
tú	riñas
él	riña
nosotros	riñamos
vosotros	riñáis
ellos	riñan

FUTURE

yo	reñiré
tú	reñirás
él	reñirá
nosotros	reñiremos
vosotros	reñiréis
ellos	reñirán

CONDITIONAL

yo	reñiría
tú	reñirías
él	reñiría
nosotros	reñiríamos
vosotros	reñiríais
ellos	reñirían

IMPERFECT

yo	reñía
tú	reñías
él	reñía
nosotros	reñíamos
vosotros	reñíais
ellos	reñían

PRETERITE

yo	reñí
tú	reñiste
él	riñó
nosotros	reñimos
vosotros	reñisteis
ellos	riñeron

resolver *to solve*

PAST PARTICIPLE
resuelto

IMPERATIVE
resuelve
resolved

GERUND
resolviendo

PRESENT

yo	resuelvo
tú	resuelves
él	resuelve
nosotros	resolvemos
vosotros	resolvéis
ellos	resuelven

PRESENT SUBJUNCTIVE

yo	resuelva
tú	resuelvas
él	resuelva
nosotros	resolvamos
vosotros	resolváis
ellos	resuelvan

FUTURE

yo	resolveré
tú	resolverás
él	resolverá
nosotros	resolveremos
vosotros	resolveréis
ellos	resolverán

CONDITIONAL

yo	resolvería
tú	resolverías
él	resolvería
nosotros	resolveríamos
vosotros	resolveríais
ellos	resolverían

IMPERFECT

yo	resolvía
tú	resolvías
él	resolvía
nosotros	resolvíamos
vosotros	resolvíais
ellos	resolvían

PRETERITE

yo	resolví
tú	resolviste
él	resolvió
nosotros	resolvimos
vosotros	resolvisteis
ellos	resolvieron

reunir *to put together, gather*

PAST PARTICIPLE
reunido

IMPERATIVE
reúne
reunid

GERUND
reuniendo

PRESENT	
yo	reúno
tú	reúnes
él	reúne
nosotros	reunimos
vosotros	reunís
ellos	reúnen

PRESENT SUBJUNCTIVE	
yo	reúna
tú	reúnas
él	reúna
nosotros	reunamos
vosotros	reunáis
ellos	reúnan

FUTURE	
yo	reuniré
tú	reunirás
él	reunirá
nosotros	reuniremos
vosotros	reuniréis
ellos	reunirán

CONDITIONAL	
yo	reuniría
tú	reunirías
él	reuniría
nosotros	reuniríamos
vosotros	reuniríais
ellos	reunirían

IMPERFECT	
yo	reunía
tú	reunías
él	reunía
nosotros	reuníamos
vosotros	reuníais
ellos	reunían

PRETERITE	
yo	reuní
tú	reuniste
él	reunió
nosotros	reunimos
vosotros	reunisteis
ellos	reunieron

rogar *to beg*

PAST PARTICIPLE
rogado

GERUND
rogando

IMPERATIVE
ruega
rogad

PRESENT

yo	ruego
tú	ruegas
él	ruega
nosotros	rogamos
vosotros	rogáis
ellos	ruegan

FUTURE

yo	rogaré
tú	rogarás
él	rogará
nosotros	rogaremos
vosotros	rogaréis
ellos	rogarán

IMPERFECT

yo	rogaba
tú	rogabas
él	rogaba
nosotros	rogábamos
vosotros	rogabais
ellos	rogaban

PRESENT SUBJUNCTIVE

yo	ruegue
tú	ruegues
él	ruegue
nosotros	roguemos
vosotros	roguéis
ellos	rueguen

CONDITIONAL

yo	rogaría
tú	rogarías
él	rogaría
nosotros	rogaríamos
vosotros	rogaríais
ellos	rogarían

PRETERITE

yo	rogué
tú	rogaste
él	rogó
nosotros	rogamos
vosotros	rogasteis
ellos	rogaron

romper *to break*

PAST PARTICIPLE
roto

IMPERATIVE
rompe
romped

GERUND
rompiendo

PRESENT

yo	rompo
tú	rompes
él	rompe
nosotros	rompemos
vosotros	rompéis
ellos	rompen

PRESENT SUBJUNCTIVE

yo	rompa
tú	rompas
él	rompa
nosotros	rompamos
vosotros	rompáis
ellos	rompan

FUTURE

yo	romperé
tú	romperás
él	romperá
nosotros	romperemos
vosotros	romperéis
ellos	romperán

CONDITIONAL

yo	rompería
tú	romperías
él	rompería
nosotros	romperíamos
vosotros	romperíais
ellos	romperían

IMPERFECT

yo	rompía
tú	rompías
él	rompía
nosotros	rompíamos
vosotros	rompíais
ellos	rompían

PRETERITE

yo	rompí
tú	rompiste
él	rompió
nosotros	rompimos
vosotros	rompisteis
ellos	rompieron

saber *to know*

PAST PARTICIPLE
  sabido

GERUND
  sabiendo

IMPERATIVE
  sabe
  sabed

PRESENT
yo	sé
tú	sabes
él	sabe
nosotros	sabemos
vosotros	sabéis
ellos	saben

FUTURE
yo	sabré
tú	sabrás
él	sabrá
nosotros	sabremos
vosotros	sabréis
ellos	sabrán

IMPERFECT
yo	sabía
tú	sabías
él	sabía
nosotros	sabíamos
vosotros	sabíais
ellos	sabían

PRESENT SUBJUNCTIVE
yo	sepa
tú	sepas
él	sepa
nosotros	sepamos
vosotros	sepáis
ellos	sepan

CONDITIONAL
yo	sabría
tú	sabrías
él	sabría
nosotros	sabríamos
vosotros	sabríais
ellos	sabrían

PRETERITE
yo	supe
tú	supiste
él	supo
nosotros	supimos
vosotros	supisteis
ellos	supieron

sacar *to take out*

PAST PARTICIPLE
sacado

IMPERATIVE
saca
sacad

GERUND
sacando

PRESENT		PRESENT SUBJUNCTIVE	
yo	saco	yo	saque
tú	sacas	tú	saques
él	saca	él	saque
nosotros	sacamos	nosotros	saquemos
vosotros	sacáis	vosotros	saquéis
ellos	sacan	ellos	saquen

FUTURE		CONDITIONAL	
yo	sacaré	yo	sacaría
tú	sacarás	tú	sacarías
él	sacará	él	sacaría
nosotros	sacaremos	nosotros	sacaríamos
vosotros	sacaréis	vosotros	sacaríais
ellos	sacarán	ellos	sacarían

IMPERFECT		PRETERITE	
yo	sacaba	yo	saqué
tú	sacabas	tú	sacaste
él	sacaba	él	sacó
nosotros	sacábamos	nosotros	sacamos
vosotros	sacabais	vosotros	sacasteis
ellos	sacaban	ellos	sacaron

salir *to go out*

PAST PARTICIPLE
salido

GERUND
saliendo

IMPERATIVE
sal
salid

PRESENT

yo	salgo
tú	sales
él	sale
nosotros	salimos
vosotros	salís
ellos	salen

FUTURE

yo	saldré
tú	saldrás
él	saldrá
nosotros	saldremos
vosotros	saldréis
ellos	saldrán

IMPERFECT

yo	salía
tú	salías
él	salía
nosotros	salíamos
vosotros	salíais
ellos	salían

PRESENT SUBJUNCTIVE

yo	salga
tú	salgas
él	salga
nosotros	salgamos
vosotros	salgáis
ellos	salgan

CONDITIONAL

yo	saldría
tú	saldrías
él	saldría
nosotros	saldríamos
vosotros	saldríais
ellos	saldrían

PRETERITE

yo	salí
tú	saliste
él	salió
nosotros	salimos
vosotros	salisteis
ellos	salieron

satisfacer *to satisfy*

PAST PARTICIPLE
satisfecho

GERUND
satisfaciendo

IMPERATIVE
satisfaz/satisface
satisfaced

PRESENT		*PRESENT SUBJUNCTIVE*	
yo	satisfago	yo	satisfaga
tú	satisfaces	tú	satisfagas
él	satisface	él	satisfaga
nosotros	satisfacemos	nosotros	satisfagamos
vosotros	satisfacéis	vosotros	satisfagáis
ellos	satisfacen	ellos	satisfagan

FUTURE		*CONDITIONAL*	
yo	satisfaré	yo	satisfaría
tú	satisfarás	tú	satisfarías
él	satisfará	él	satisfaría
nosotros	satisfaremos	nosotros	satisfaríamos
vosotros	satisfaréis	vosotros	satisfaríais
ellos	satisfarán	ellos	satisfarían

IMPERFECT		*PRETERITE*	
yo	satisfacía	yo	satisfice
tú	satisfacías	tú	satisficiste
él	satisfacía	él	satisfizo
nosotros	satisfacíamos	nosotros	satisficimos
vosotros	satisfacíais	vosotros	satisficisteis
ellos	satisfacían	ellos	satisficieron

seguir *to follow*

PAST PARTICIPLE
segu**ido**

IMPERATIVE
sigue
segui**d**

GERUND
siguiendo

PRESENT	
yo	sigo
tú	sigues
él	sigue
nosotros	segu**imos**
vosotros	segu**ís**
ellos	siguen

PRESENT SUBJUNCTIVE	
yo	siga
tú	sigas
él	siga
nosotros	sigamos
vosotros	sigáis
ellos	sigan

FUTURE	
yo	seguir**é**
tú	seguir**ás**
él	seguir**á**
nosotros	seguir**emos**
vosotros	seguir**éis**
ellos	seguir**án**

CONDITIONAL	
yo	seguir**ía**
tú	seguir**ías**
él	seguir**ía**
nosotros	seguir**íamos**
vosotros	seguir**íais**
ellos	seguir**ían**

IMPERFECT	
yo	segu**ía**
tú	segu**ías**
él	segu**ía**
nosotros	segu**íamos**
vosotros	segu**íais**
ellos	segu**ían**

PRETERITE	
yo	segu**í**
tú	segu**iste**
él	siguió
nosotros	segu**imos**
vosotros	segu**isteis**
ellos	siguieron

sentir *to feel*

PAST PARTICIPLE
sentido

GERUND
sintiendo

IMPERATIVE
siente
sentid

PRESENT
yo	siento
tú	sientes
él	siente
nosotros	sentimos
vosotros	sentís
ellos	sienten

PRESENT SUBJUNCTIVE
yo	sienta
tú	sientas
él	sienta
nosotros	sintamos
vosotros	sintáis
ellos	sientan

FUTURE
yo	sentiré
tú	sentirás
él	sentirá
nosotros	sentiremos
vosotros	sentiréis
ellos	sentirán

CONDITIONAL
yo	sentiría
tú	sentirías
él	sentiría
nosotros	sentiríamos
vosotros	sentiríais
ellos	sentirían

IMPERFECT
yo	sentía
tú	sentías
él	sentía
nosotros	sentíamos
vosotros	sentíais
ellos	sentían

PRETERITE
yo	sentí
tú	sentiste
él	sintió
nosotros	sentimos
vosotros	sentisteis
ellos	sintieron

ser *to be*

PAST PARTICIPLE
sido

GERUND
siendo

IMPERATIVE
sé
sed

PRESENT

yo	soy
tú	eres
él	es
nosotros	somos
vosotros	sois
ellos	son

FUTURE

yo	seré
tú	serás
él	será
nosotros	seremos
vosotros	seréis
ellos	serán

IMPERFECT

yo	era
tú	eras
él	era
nosotros	éramos
vosotros	erais
ellos	eran

PRESENT SUBJUNCTIVE

yo	sea
tú	seas
él	sea
nosotros	seamos
vosotros	seáis
ellos	sean

CONDITIONAL

yo	sería
tú	serías
él	sería
nosotros	seríamos
vosotros	seríais
ellos	serían

PRETERITE

yo	fui
tú	fuiste
él	fue
nosotros	fuimos
vosotros	fuisteis
ellos	fueron

tener *to have*

PAST PARTICIPLE
  tenido

GERUND
  teniendo

IMPERATIVE
  ten
  tened

PRESENT
yo	tengo
tú	tienes
él	tiene
nosotros	tenemos
vosotros	tenéis
ellos	tienen

PRESENT SUBJUNCTIVE
yo	tenga
tú	tengas
él	tenga
nosotros	tengamos
vosotros	tengáis
ellos	tengan

FUTURE
yo	tendré
tú	tendrás
él	tendrá
nosotros	tendremos
vosotros	tendréis
ellos	tendrán

CONDITIONAL
yo	tendría
tú	tendrías
él	tendría
nosotros	tendríamos
vosotros	tendríais
ellos	tendrían

IMPERFECT
yo	tenía
tú	tenías
él	tenía
nosotros	teníamos
vosotros	teníais
ellos	tenían

PRETERITE
yo	tuve
tú	tuviste
él	tuvo
nosotros	tuvimos
vosotros	tuvisteis
ellos	tuvieron

torcer *to twist*

PAST PARTICIPLE
torcido

GERUND
torciendo

IMPERATIVE
tuerce
torced

PRESENT		PRESENT SUBJUNCTIVE	
yo	tuerzo	yo	tuerza
tú	tuerces	tú	tuerzas
él	tuerce	él	tuerza
nosotros	torcemos	nosotros	torzamos
vosotros	torcéis	vosotros	torzáis
ellos	tuercen	ellos	tuerzan

FUTURE		CONDITIONAL	
yo	torceré	yo	torcería
tú	torcerás	tú	torcerías
él	torcerá	él	torcería
nosotros	torceremos	nosotros	torceríamos
vosotros	torceréis	vosotros	torceríais
ellos	torcerán	ellos	torcerían

IMPERFECT		PRETERITE	
yo	torcía	yo	torcí
tú	torcías	tú	torciste
él	torcía	él	torció
nosotros	torcíamos	nosotros	torcimos
vosotros	torcíais	vosotros	torcisteis
ellos	torcían	ellos	torcieron

traer *to bring*

PAST PARTICIPLE
traído

IMPERATIVE
trae
traed

GERUND
trayendo

PRESENT

yo	traigo
tú	traes
él	trae
nosotros	traemos
vosotros	traéis
ellos	traen

PRESENT SUBJUNCTIVE

yo	traiga
tú	traigas
él	traiga
nosotros	traigamos
vosotros	traigáis
ellos	traigan

FUTURE

yo	traeré
tú	traerás
él	traerá
nosotros	traeremos
vosotros	traeréis
ellos	traerán

CONDITIONAL

yo	traería
tú	traerías
él	traería
nosotros	traeríamos
vosotros	traeríais
ellos	traerían

IMPERFECT

yo	traía
tú	traías
él	traía
nosotros	traíamos
vosotros	traíais
ellos	traían

PRETERITE

yo	traje
tú	trajiste
él	trajo
nosotros	trajimos
vosotros	trajisteis
ellos	trajeron

valer *to be worth*

PAST PARTICIPLE
valido

IMPERATIVE
vale
valed

GERUND
valiendo

PRESENT
yo	valgo
tú	vales
él	vale
nosotros	valemos
vosotros	valéis
ellos	valen

FUTURE
yo	valdré
tú	valdrás
él	valdrá
nosotros	valdremos
vosotros	valdréis
ellos	valdrán

IMPERFECT
yo	valía
tú	valías
él	valía
nosotros	valíamos
vosotros	valíais
ellos	valían

PRESENT SUBJUNCTIVE
yo	valga
tú	valgas
él	valga
nosotros	valgamos
vosotros	valgáis
ellos	valgan

CONDITIONAL
yo	valdría
tú	valdrías
él	valdría
nosotros	valdríamos
vosotros	valdríais
ellos	valdrían

PRETERITE
yo	valí
tú	valiste
él	valió
nosotros	valimos
vosotros	valisteis
ellos	valieron

vencer *to win*

PAST PARTICIPLE
vencido

IMPERATIVE
vence
venced

GERUND
venciendo

PRESENT
yo	venzo
tú	vences
él	vence
nosotros	vencemos
vosotros	vencéis
ellos	vencen

PRESENT SUBJUNCTIVE
yo	venza
tú	venzas
él	venza
nosotros	venzamos
vosotros	venzáis
ellos	venzan

FUTURE
yo	venceré
tú	vencerás
él	vencerá
nosotros	venceremos
vosotros	venceréis
ellos	vencerán

CONDITIONAL
yo	vencería
tú	vencerías
él	vencería
nosotros	venceríamos
vosotros	venceríais
ellos	vencerían

IMPERFECT
yo	vencía
tú	vencías
él	vencía
nosotros	vencíamos
vosotros	vencíais
ellos	vencían

PRETERITE
yo	vencí
tú	venciste
él	venció
nosotros	vencimos
vosotros	vencisteis
ellos	vencieron

venir *to come*

PAST PARTICIPLE
venido

IMPERATIVE
ven
venid

GERUND
viniendo

PRESENT		*PRESENT SUBJUNCTIVE*	
yo	vengo	yo	venga
tú	vienes	tú	vengas
él	viene	él	venga
nosotros	venimos	nosotros	vengamos
vosotros	venís	vosotros	vengáis
ellos	vienen	ellos	vengan

FUTURE		*CONDITIONAL*	
yo	vendré	yo	vendría
tú	vendrás	tú	vendrías
él	vendrá	él	vendría
nosotros	vendremos	nosotros	vendríamos
vosotros	vendréis	vosotros	vendríais
ellos	vendrán	ellos	vendrían

IMPERFECT		*PRETERITE*	
yo	venía	yo	vine
tú	venías	tú	viniste
él	venía	él	vino
nosotros	veníamos	nosotros	vinimos
vosotros	veníais	vosotros	vinisteis
ellos	venían	ellos	vinieron

ver *to see*

PAST PARTICIPLE
visto

IMPERATIVE
ve
ved

GERUND
viendo

PRESENT			PRESENT SUBJUNCTIVE	
yo	veo		yo	vea
tú	ves		tú	veas
él	ve		él	vea
nosotros	vemos		nosotros	veamos
vosotros	veis		vosotros	veáis
ellos	ven		ellos	vean

FUTURE			CONDITIONAL	
yo	veré		yo	vería
tú	verás		tú	verías
él	verá		él	vería
nosotros	veremos		nosotros	veríamos
vosotros	veréis		vosotros	veríais
ellos	verán		ellos	verían

IMPERFECT			PRETERITE	
yo	veía		yo	vi
tú	veías		tú	viste
él	veía		él	vio
nosotros	veíamos		nosotros	vimos
vosotros	veíais		vosotros	visteis
ellos	veían		ellos	vieron

volcar *to overturn*

PAST PARTICIPLE
volcado

IMPERATIVE
vuelca
volcad

GERUND
volcando

PRESENT

yo	**vuelco**
tú	**vuelcas**
él	**vuelca**
nosotros	volcamos
vosotros	volcáis
ellos	**vuelcan**

FUTURE

yo	volcaré
tú	volcarás
él	volcará
nosotros	volcaremos
vosotros	volcaréis
ellos	volcarán

IMPERFECT

yo	volcaba
tú	volcabas
él	volcaba
nosotros	volcábamos
vosotros	volcabais
ellos	volcaban

PRESENT SUBJUNCTIVE

yo	**vuelque**
tú	**vuelques**
él	**vuelque**
nosotros	**volquemos**
vosotros	**volquéis**
ellos	**vuelquen**

CONDITIONAL

yo	volcaría
tú	volcarías
él	volcaría
nosotros	volcaríamos
vosotros	volcaríais
ellos	volcarían

PRETERITE

yo	volqué
tú	volcaste
él	volcó
nosotros	volcamos
vosotros	volcasteis
ellos	volcaron

160 VERBS: IRREGULAR

volver *to return*

PAST PARTICIPLE
vuelto

GERUND
volviendo

IMPERATIVE
vuelve
volved

PRESENT

yo	vuelvo
tú	vuelves
él	vuelve
nosotros	volvemos
vosotros	volvéis
ellos	vuelven

FUTURE

yo	volveré
tú	volverás
él	volverá
nosotros	volveremos
vosotros	volveréis
ellos	volverán

IMPERFECT

yo	volvía
tú	volvías
él	volvía
nosotros	volvíamos
vosotros	volvíais
ellos	volvían

PRESENT SUBJUNCTIVE

yo	vuelva
tú	vuelvas
él	vuelva
nosotros	volvamos
vosotros	volváis
ellos	vuelvan

CONDITIONAL

yo	volvería
tú	volverías
él	volvería
nosotros	volveríamos
vosotros	volveríais
ellos	volverían

PRETERITE

yo	volví
tú	volviste
él	volvió
nosotros	volvimos
vosotros	volvisteis
ellos	volvieron

zurcir *to darn*

PAST PARTICIPLE	*IMPERATIVE*
zurcido	zurce
	zurcid
GERUND	
zurciendo	

PRESENT		*PRESENT SUBJUNCTIVE*	
yo	zurzo	yo	zurza
tú	zurces	tú	zurzas
él	zurce	él	zurza
nosotros	zurcimos	nosotros	zurzamos
vosotros	zurcís	vosotros	zurzáis
ellos	zurcen	ellos	zurzan

FUTURE		*CONDITIONAL*	
yo	zurciré	yo	zurciría
tú	zurcirás	tú	zurcirías
él	zurcirá	él	zurciría
nosotros	zurciremos	nosotros	zurciríamos
vosotros	zurciréis	vosotros	zurciríais
ellos	zurcirán	ellos	zurcirían

IMPERFECT		*PRETERITE*	
yo	zurcía	yo	zurcí
tú	zurcías	tú	zurciste
él	zurcía	él	zurció
nosotros	zurcíamos	nosotros	zurcimos
vosotros	zurcíais	vosotros	zurcisteis
ellos	zurcían	ellos	zurcieron

The following pages, 163 to 186, contain an index of over 2,800 commonly used verbs cross-referred to the appropriate conjugation model.

- Regular verbs belonging to the first, second and third conjugation are numbered 1, 2 and 3 respectively. For the regular conjugations see pp 6 to 13.

- Irregular verbs are numerically cross-referred to the appropriate model as conjugated on pp 82 to 161. Thus, **alzar** is cross-referred to p 100 where **cruzar**, the model for this verb group, is conjugated.

- Verbs which are most commonly used in the reflexive form — e.g. **amodorrarse** — have been cross-referred to the appropriate non-reflexive model. For the full conjugation of a reflexive verb, see pp 28 to 31.

- Verbs printed in colour — e.g. abrir — are themselves models.

- Superior numbers refer you to notes on p 187 which indicate how the verb differs from its model.

abalanzar	100	acaecer[1]	99	acostumbrar	1
abandonar	1	acalorarse	1	acrecentar	133
abanicar	146	acampar	1	acreditar	1
abaratar	1	acaparar	1	acribillar	1
abarcar	146	acariciar	1	activar	1
abarrotar	1	acarrear	1	actualizar	100
abastecer	99	acatar	1	**actuar**	84
abatir	3	acatarrarse	1	acuciar	1
abdicar	146	acaudalar	1	acuclillarse	1
abjurar	1	acaudillar	1	acudir	3
ablandar	1	acceder	2	acumular	1
abnegarse	128	accidentarse	1	acuñar	1
abocar	146	accionar	1	acurrucarse	1
abochornar	1	acelerar	1	acusar	1
abofetear	1	acentuar	84	achacar	146
abogar	131	aceptar	1	achicar	146
abolir	82	acercar	146	achicharrar	1
abollar	1	acertar	133	adaptar	1
abombar	1	acicalar	1	adecuar	1
abonar	1	aclamar	1	adelantar	1
abordar	1	aclarar	1	adelgazar	100
aborrecer	99	aclimatar	1	aderezar	100
abortar	1	acobardarse	1	adeudar	1
abotonar	1	acodarse	1	adherirse	150
abrasar	1	acoger	95	adicionar	1
abrazar	100	acolchar	1	adiestrar	1
abreviar	1	acometer	2	adivinar	1
abrigar	131	acomodar	1	adjudicar	146
abrir	83	acompañar	1	adjuntar	1
abrochar	1	acomplejar	1	administrar	1
abrumar	1	acondicionar	1	admirar	1
absolver	160	acongojar	1	admitir	3
absorber	2	aconsejar	1	adoctrinar	1
abstenerse	152	acontecer[1]	99	adolecer	99
abstraer	154	acoplar	1	adoptar	1
abultar	1	acordar	98	adorar	1
abundar	1	acorralar	1	adormecer	99
aburrir	3	acortar	1	adornar	1
abusar	1	acosar	1	adosar	1
acabar	1	acostar	98	**adquirir**	85

Notes

The notes below indicate special peculiarities of individual verbs. When only some forms of a given tense are affected, all these are shown. When all forms of the tense are affected, only the 1st and 2nd persons are shown, followed by *etc*.

1 Gerund *2* Past Participle *3* Present *4* Preterite *5* Present Subjunctive *6* Imperfect Subjunctive

1) **acaecer, acontecer, amanecer, anochecer, competer, deshelar, escampar, granizar, helar, nevar, nublarse, relampaguear, tronar, verdear, verdecer:** used almost exclusively in infinitive and 3rd person singular

2) **asir** *3* asgo *5* asga, asgas *etc*

3) **atañer** *1* atañendo *4* atañó: see also 1) above

4) **balbucir** *3* balbuceo *5* balbucee, balbucees *etc*

5) **concernir** *3* concierne, conciernen *5* concierna, conciernan: only used in 3rd person

6) **degollar** *3* degüello, degüellas, degüella, degüellan *5* degüelle, degüelles, degüellen

7) **delinquir** *3* delinco *5* delinca, delincas *etc*

8) **desasir** *3* desasgo *5* desasga, desasgas *etc*

9) **discernir** *3* discierno, disciernes, discierne, disciernen *5* discierna, disciernas, disciernan

10) **enraizar** *3* enraízo, enraízas, enraíza, enraízan *5* enraíce, enraíces, enraícen

11) **pudrir** *2* podrido

12) **rehuir** *3* rehúyo, rehúyes, rehúye, rehúyen *5* rehúya, rehúyas, rehúyan

13) **roer** *4* royó, royeron *6* royera, royeras *etc*

14) **soler:** used only in present and imperfect indicative

15) **yacer** *3* yazgo *or* yazco *or* yago *5* yazga *etc or* yazca *etc or* yaga *etc*

The Gender of Nouns

In Spanish, all nouns are either masculine or feminine, whether denoting people, animals or things. Gender is largely unpredictable and has to be learnt for each noun. However, the following guidelines will help you determine the gender for certain types of nouns.

● Nouns denoting male people and animals are usually — but not always — masculine, e.g.

un hombre	**un toro**
a man	*a bull*
un enfermero	**un semental**
a (male) nurse	*a stallion*

● Nouns denoting female people and animals are usually — but not always — feminine, e.g.

una niña	**una vaca**
a girl	*a cow*
una enfermera	**una yegua**
a nurse	*a mare*

● Some nouns are masculine *or* feminine depending on the sex of the person to whom they refer, e.g.

un camarada	**una camarada**
a (male) comrade	*a (female) comrade*
un belga	**una belga**
a Belgian (man)	*a Belgian (woman)*
un marroquí	**una marroquí**
a Moroccan (man)	*a Moroccan (woman)*

● Other nouns referring to either men or women have only one gender which applies to both, e.g.

una persona	**una visita**
a person	*a visitor*
una víctima	**una estrella**
a victim	*a star*

• Often the ending of a noun indicates its gender. Shown below are some of the most important to guide you.

Masculine endings

-o	**un clavo** *a nail*, **un plátano** *a banana* *EXCEPTIONS*: **mano** *hand*, **foto** *photograph*, **moto(cicleta)** *motorbike*
-l	**un tonel** *a barrel*, **un hotel** *a hotel* *EXCEPTIONS*: **cal** *lime*, **cárcel** *prison*, **catedral** *cathedral*, **col** *cabbage*, **miel** *honey*, **piel** *skin*, **sal** *salt*, **señal** *sign*
-r	**un tractor** *a tractor*, **el altar** *the altar* *EXCEPTIONS*: **coliflor** *cauliflower*, **flor** *flower*, **labor** *task*
-y	**el rey** *the king*, **un buey** *an ox* *EXCEPTION*: **ley** *law*

Feminine endings

-a	**una casa** *a house*, **la cara** *the face* *EXCEPTIONS*: **día** *day*, **mapa** *map*, **planeta** *planet*, **tranvía** *tram*, and most words ending in **-ma** (**tema** *subject*, **problema** *problem*, etc)
-ión	**una canción** *a song*, **una procesión** *a procession* *EXCEPTIONS*: most nouns not ending in **-ción** or **-sión**, e.g. **avión** *aeroplane*, **camión** *lorry*, **gorrión** sparrow
-dad, -tad, -tud	**una ciudad** *a town*, **la libertad** *freedom*, **una multitud** a crowd
-ed	**una pared** *a wall*, **la sed** *thirst* *EXCEPTION*: **césped** *lawn*
-itis	**una faringitis** *pharyngitis*, **la celulitis** *cellulitis*
-iz	**una perdiz** *a partridge*, **una matriz** *a matrix* *EXCEPTIONS*: **lápiz** *pencil*, **maíz** *corn*, **tapiz** *tapestry*
-sis	**una tesis** *a thesis*, **una dosis** *a dose* *EXCEPTIONS*: **análisis** *analysis*, **énfasis** *emphasis*, **paréntesis** *parenthesis*
-umbre	**la podredumbre** *rot*, **la muchedumbre** *crowd*

Gender of nouns (contd)

Some nouns change meaning according to gender. The most common are set out below:

	MASCULINE	FEMININE	
capital	*capital* (money)	*capital* (city)	(→1)
clave	*harpsichord*	*clue*	
cólera	*cholera*	*anger*	(→2)
cometa	*comet*	*kite*	
corriente	*current month*	*current*	
corte	*cut*	*court* (royal)	(→3)
coma	*coma*	*comma*	(→4)
cura	*priest*	*cure*	(→5)
frente	*front* (in war)	*forehead*	(→6)
guardia	*guard(sman)*	*guard*	(→7)
guía	*guide* (person)	*guide(book)*	(→8)
moral	*mulberry tree*	*morals*	
orden	*order* (arrangement)	*order* (command)	(→9)
ordenanza	*office boy*	*ordinance*	
papa	*Pope*	*potato*	
parte	*dispatch*	*part*	(→10)
pendiente	*earring*	*slope*	
pez	*fish*	*pitch*	
policía	*policeman*	*police*	
radio	*radius, radium*	*radio*	

1 **Invirtieron mucho capital**
   They invested a lot of capital
   La capital es muy fea
   The capital city is very ugly

2 **Es difícil luchar contra el cólera**   **Montó en cólera**
   Cholera is difficult to combat   He got angry

3 **Me encanta tu corte de pelo**
   I love your haircut
   Se trasladó la corte a Madrid
   The court was moved to Madrid

4 **Entró en un coma profundo**
   He went into a deep coma
   Aquí hace falta una coma
   You need to put a comma here

5 **¿Quién es? — El cura**   **No tiene cura**
   Who is it? — The priest   It's hopeless

6 **Han mandado a su hijo al frente**
   Her son has been sent to the front
   Tiene la frente muy ancha
   She has a very broad forehead

7 **Vino un guardia de tráfico**
   A traffic policeman came
   Están relevando la guardia ahora
   They're changing the guard now

8 **Nuestro guía nos hizo reír a carcajadas**
   Our guide had us falling about laughing
   Busco una guía turística
   I'm looking for a guidebook

9 **Están en orden alfabético**
   They're in alphabetical order
   No hemos recibido la orden de pago
   We haven't had the payment order

10 **Le mandó un parte al general**
   He sent a dispatch to the general
   En alguna parte debe estar
   It must be somewhere or other

Gender: the formation of feminines

As in English, male and female are sometimes differentiated by the use of two quite separate words, e.g.

mi marido	**mi mujer**
my husband	*my wife*
un toro	**una vaca**
a bull	*a cow*

There are, however, some words in Spanish which show this distinction by the form of their ending

- Nouns ending in **-o** change to **-a** to form the feminine (→1)

- If the masculine singular form already ends in **-a**, no further **-a** is added to the feminine (→2)

- If the last letter of the masculine singular form is a consonant, an **-a** is normally added in the feminine* (→3)

Feminine forms to note

MASCULINE	FEMININE	
el abad	**la abadesa**	*abbot/abbess*
un actor	**una actriz**	*actor/actress*
el alcalde	**la alcaldesa**	*mayor/mayoress*
el conde	**la condesa**	*count/countess*
el duque	**la duquesa**	*duke/duchess*
el emperador	**la emperatriz**	*emperor/empress*
un poeta	**una poetisa**	*poet/poetess*
el príncipe	**la princesa**	*prince/princess*
el rey	**la reina**	*king/queen*
un sacerdote	**una sacerdotisa**	*priest/priestess*
un tigre	**una tigresa**	*tiger/tigress*
el zar	**la zarina**	*tzar/tzarina*

*If the last syllable has an accent, it disappears in the feminine (see p 292) (→4)

1 **un amigo**
   a (male) friend
   un empleado
   a (male) employee
   un gato
   a cat

   una amiga
   a (female) friend
   una empleada
   a (female) employee
   una gata
   a (female) cat

2 **un deportista**
   a sportsman
   un colega
   a (male) colleague
   un camarada
   a (male) comrade

   una deportista
   a sportswoman
   una colega
   a (female) colleague
   una camarada
   a (female) comrade

3 **un español**
   a Spaniard, a Spanish man
   un vendedor
   a salesman
   un jugador
   a (male) player

   una española
   a Spanish woman
   una vendedora
   a saleswoman
   una jugadora
   a (female) player

4 **un lapón**
   a Laplander (man)
   un león
   a lion
   un neocelandés
   a New Zealander (man)

   una lapona
   a Laplander (woman)
   una leona
   a lioness
   una neocelandesa
   a New Zealander (woman)

The formation of plurals

- Nouns ending in an unstressed vowel add **-s** to the singular form (→**1**)

- Nouns ending in a consonant or a stressed vowel add **-es** to the singular form (→**2**)

  EXCEPTIONS:

café	*coffee shop*	(plur: **cafés**)
mamá	*mummy*	(plur: **mamás**)
papá	*daddy*	(plur: **papás**)
pie	*foot*	(plur: **pies**)
sofá	*sofa*	(plur: **sofás**)
té	*tea*	(plur: **tes**)

  and words of foreign origin ending in a consonant, e.g.:

coñac	*brandy*	(plur: **coñacs**)
jersey	*jumper*	(plur: **jerseys**)

  It should be noted that:
  - nouns ending in **-n** or **-s** with an accent on the last syllable drop this accent in the plural (see p 292) (→**3**)
  - nouns ending in **-n** with the stress on the second-last syllable in the singular add an accent to that syllable in the plural in order to show the correct position for stress (see p 292) (→**4**)
  - nouns ending in **-z** change this to **c** in the plural (→**5**)

- Nouns with an unstressed final syllable ending in **-s** do not change in the plural (→**6**)

1 **la casa**   **las casas**
   the house   the houses
   el libro   **los libros**
   the book   the books

2 **un rumor**   **unos rumores**
   a rumour   (some) rumours
   un jabalí   **unos jabalíes**
   a boar   (some) boars

3 **la canción**   **las canciones**
   the song   the songs
   el autobús   **los autobuses**
   the bus   the buses

4 **un examen**   **unos exámenes**
   an exam   (some) exams
   un crimen   **unos crímenes**
   a crime   (some) crimes

5 **la luz**   **las luces**
   the light   the lights

6 **un paraguas**   **unos paraguas**
   an umbrella   (some) umbrellas
   la dosis   **las dosis**
   the dose   the doses
   el lunes   **los lunes**
   Monday   Mondays

The Definite Article

	WITH MASC NOUN	WITH FEM NOUN	
SING	**el**	**la**	*the*
PLUR	**los**	**las**	*the*

- The gender and number of the noun determine the form of the article ($\rightarrow$1)

  It should be noted, however, that if the article comes directly before a feminine singular noun which starts with a stressed **a-** or **ha-**, the masculine form **el** is used instead of the feminine **la** ($\rightarrow$2)

- For uses of the definite article see p 199

- **a** + **el** becomes **al** ($\rightarrow$3)

- **de** + **el** becomes **del** ($\rightarrow$4)

Continued

1 el **tren**   la **estación**
   the train   the station
   el **actor**   la **actriz**
   the actor   the actress
   los **hoteles**   las **escuelas**
   the hotels   the schools
   los **profesores**   las **mujeres**
   the teachers   the women

2 el **agua**   *but*   la **misma agua**
   the water   the same water
   el **hacha**   *but*   la **mejor hacha**
   the axe   the best axe

3 al **cine**
   to the cinema
   al **empleado**
   to the employee
   al **hospital**
   to the hospital

4 del **departamento**
   from/of the department
   del **autor**
   from/of the author
   del **presidente**
   from/of the president

Uses of the definite article

While the definite article is used in much the same way in Spanish as it is in English, its use is more widespread in Spanish. Unlike English the definite article is also used:

- with abstract nouns, except when following certain prepositions (→**1**)

- in generalizations, especially with plural or uncountable* nouns (→**2**)

- with parts of the body (→**3**)
  'Ownership' is often indicated by an indirect object pronoun or a reflexive pronoun (→**4**)

- with titles/ranks/professions followed by a proper name (→**5**)
  EXCEPTIONS: with **Don/Doña, San/Santo(a)** (→**6**)

- before nouns of official, academic and religious buildings, and names of meals and games (→**7**)

- The definite article is *NOT* used with nouns in apposition unless those nouns are individualized (→**8**)

*An uncountable noun is one which cannot be used in the plural or with an indefinite article, e.g. **el acero** *steel*, **la leche** *milk*.

1 **Los precios suben**
 Prices are rising
 El tiempo es oro
 Time is money
 but
 con pasión   sin esperanza
 with passion   without hope
2 **No me gusta el café**
 I don't like coffee
 Los niños necesitan ser queridos
 Children need to be loved
3 **Vuelva la cabeza hacia la izquierda**
 Turn your head to the left
 No puedo mover las piernas
 I can't move my legs
4 **La cabeza me da vueltas**
 My head is spinning
 Lávate las manos
 Wash your hands
5 **El rey Jorge III   el capitán Menéndez**
 King George III   Captain Menéndez
 el doctor Ochoa   el señor Ramírez
 Doctor Ochoa   Mr. Ramírez
6 **Don Arturo Ruiz   Santa Teresa**
 Mr. Arturo Ruiz   Saint Teresa
7 **en la cárcel   en la universidad   en la iglesia**
 in prison   at university   at church
 la cena   el tenis   el ajedrez
 dinner   tennis   chess
8 **Madrid, capital de España, es la ciudad que …**
 Madrid, the capital of Spain, is the city which …
 but
 Maria Callas, la famosa cantante de ópera …
 Maria Callas, the famous opera singer …

The Indefinite Article

	WITH MASC NOUN	WITH FEM NOUN	
SING	**un**	**una**	*a*
PLUR	**unos**	**unas**	*some*

The indefinite article is used in Spanish largely as it is in English EXCEPT:

- There is no article when a person's profession is being stated (→1)
  The article is used, however, when the profession is qualified by an adjective (→2)

- The article is not used with the following words:

otro	*another*	(→3)
cierto	*certain*	(→4)
semejante	*such (a)*	(→5)
tal	*such (a)*	(→6)
cien	*a hundred*	(→7)
mil	*a thousand*	(→8)
sin	*without*	(→9)
qué	*what a*	(→10)

- There is no article with a noun in apposition (→11). When an abstract noun is qualified by an adjective, the indefinite article is used, but is not translated in English (→12)

1 **Es profesor**   **Mi madre es enfermera**
   He's a teacher   My mother is a nurse
2 **Es un buen médico**
   He's a good doctor
   Se hizo una escritora célebre
   She became a famous writer
3 **otro libro**
   another book
4 **cierta calle**
   a certain street
5 **semejante ruido**
   such a noise
6 **tal mentira**
   such a lie
7 **cien soldados**
   a hundred soldiers
8 **mil años**
   a thousand years
9 **sin casa**
   without a house
10 **¡Qué sorpresa!**
   What a surprise!
11 **Baroja, gran escritor de la Generación del 98**
   Baroja, a great writer of the 'Generación del 98'
12 **con una gran sabiduría/un valor admirable**
   with great wisdom/admirable courage
   Dieron pruebas de una sangre fría increíble
   They showed incredible coolness
   una película de un mal gusto espantoso
   a film in appallingly bad taste

The Article 'lo'

This is never used with a noun. Instead, it is used in the following ways:

- As an intensifier before an adjective or adverb in the construction

  lo + adjective/adverb + que (→1)

  Note that the adjective agrees with the noun it refers to (→2)

- With an adjective or participle to form an abstract noun (→3)

- In the phrase **lo de** to refer to a subject of which speaker and listener are already aware. It can often be translated as *the business/affair of/about ...* (→4)

- In set expressions, the commonest of which are:

a lo mejor	*maybe, perhaps*	(→5)
a lo lejos	*in the distance*	(→6)
a lo largo de	*along, through*	(→7)
por lo menos	*at least*	(→8)
por lo tanto	*therefore, so*	(→9)
por lo visto	*apparently*	(→10)

1 **No sabíamos lo pequeña que era la casa**
We didn't know how small the house was
Sé lo mucho que te gusta la música
I know how much you like music

2 **No te imaginas lo simpáticos que son**
You can't imagine how nice they are
Ya sabes lo buenas que son estas manzanas
You already know how good these apples are

3 **Lo bueno de eso es que ...**
The good thing about it is that ...
Sentimos mucho lo ocurrido
We are very sorry about what happened

4 **Lo de ayer es mejor que lo olvides**
It's better if you forget what happened yesterday
Lo de tu hermano me preocupa mucho
The business about your brother worries me very much

5 **A lo mejor ha salido**
Perhaps he's gone out

6 **A lo lejos se veían unas casas**
Some houses could be seen in the distance

7 **A lo largo de su vida**
Throughout his life
A lo largo de la carretera
Along the road

8 **Hubo por lo menos cincuenta heridos**
At least fifty people were injured

9 **No hemos recibido ninguna instrucción al respecto, y por lo tanto no podemos ...**
We have not received any instructions about it, therefore we cannot ...

10 **Por lo visto, no viene**
Apparently he's not coming *or* He's not coming, it seems

Adjectives

Most adjectives agree in number and in gender with the noun or pronoun.
Note that:
— if the adjective refers to two or more singular nouns of the same gender, a plural ending of that gender is required (→**1**)
— if the adjective refers to two or more singular nouns of different genders, a masculine plural ending is required (→**2**)

The formation of feminines

● Adjectives ending in **-o** change to **-a** (→**3**)

● Some groups of adjectives add **-a**:
— adjectives of nationality or geographical origin (→**4**)
— adjectives ending in **-or** (except irregular comparatives: see p 210), **-án, -ón, -ín** (→**5**)
   Note: when there is an accent on the last syllable, it disappears in the feminine (see p 292)

● Other adjectives do not change (→**6**)

The formation of plurals

● Adjectives ending in an unstressed vowel add **-s** (→**7**)

● Adjectives ending in a stressed vowel or a consonant add **-es** (→**8**)
   Note that:
— if there is an accent on the last syllable of a word ending in a consonant, it will disappear in the plural (see p 292) (→**9**)
— if the last letter is a **z** it will become a **c** in the plural (→**10**)

1 **la lengua y la literatura españolas**
   (the) Spanish language and literature
2 **Nunca había visto árboles y flores tan raros**
   I had never seen such strange trees and flowers
3 **mi hermano pequeño**   **mi hermana pequeña**
   my little brother   my little sister
4 **un chico español**   **una chica española**
   a Spanish boy   a Spanish girl
   el equipo barcelonés   **la vida barcelonesa**
   the team from Barcelona   the Barcelona way of life
5 **un niño encantador**   **una niña encantadora**
   a charming little boy   a charming little girl
   un hombre holgazán   **una mujer holgazana**
   an idle man   an idle woman
   un gesto burlón   **una sonrisa burlona**
   a mocking gesture   a mocking smile
   un chico cantarín   **una chica cantarina**
   a boy fond of singing   a girl fond of singing
6 **un final feliz**   **una infancia feliz**
   a happy ending   a happy childhood
   mi amigo belga   **mi amiga belga**
   my Belgian (male) friend   my Belgian (female) friend
   el vestido verde   **la blusa verde**
   the green dress   the green blouse
7 **el último tren**   **los últimos trenes**
   the last train   the last trains
   una casa vieja   **unas casas viejas**
   an old house   (some) old houses
8 **un médico iraní**   **unos médicos iraníes**
   an Iranian doctor   (some) Iranian doctors
   un examen fácil   **unos exámenes fáciles**
   an easy exam   (some) easy exams
9 **un río francés**   **unos ríos franceses**
   a French river   (some) French rivers
10 **un día feliz**   **unos días felices**
   a happy day   (some) happy days

206 ADJECTIVES

Invariable Adjectives

Some adjectives and other parts of speech when used adjectivally never change in the feminine or plural.
The commonest of these are:
- nouns denoting colour (→1)
- compound adjectives (→2)
- nouns used as adjectives (→3)

Shortening of Adjectives

- The following drop the final **-o** before a masculine singular noun:
  bueno   *good* (→4)
  malo   *bad*
  alguno*   *some* (→5)
  ninguno*   *none*
  uno   *one* (→6)
  primero   *first* (→7)
  tercero   *third*
  postrero   *last* (→8)

*Note that an accent is required to show the correct position for stress.

- **Grande** *big, great* is usually shortened to **gran** before a masculine *or* feminine singular noun (→9)

- **Santo** *Saint* changes to **San** except with saints' names beginning with **Do-** or **To-** (→10)

- **Ciento** *a hundred* is shortened to **cien** before a masculine *or* feminine plural noun (→11)

- **Cualquiera** drops the final **-a** before a masculine *or* feminine singular noun (→12)

1 **los vestidos** naranja
the orange dresses

2 **las chaquetas** azul marino
the navy blue jackets

3 **bebés** probeta   **mujeres** soldado
test-tube babies   women soldiers

4 **un** buen **libro**
a good book

5 algún **libro**
some book

6 cuarenta y un **años**
forty-one years

7 **el** primer **hijo**
the first child

8 **un** postrer **deseo**
a last wish

9 **un** gran **actor**   **una** gran **decepción**
a great actor   a great disappointment

10 San **Antonio**   Santo To**más**
Saint Anthony   Saint Thomas

11 cien **años**
a hundred years
cien **millones**
a hundred million

12 cualquier **día**   a cualquier **hora**
any day   any time

Comparatives and Superlatives

Comparatives

These are formed using the following constructions:

más ... (que)	*more ... (than)*	(→1)
menos ... (que)	*less ... (than)*	(→2)
tanto ... como	*as ... as*	(→3)
tan ... como	*as ... as*	(→4)
tan ... que	*so ... that*	(→5)
demasiado ... ⎫	*too ...* ⎫	
bastante ... ⎬ **para**	*enough ...* ⎬ *to*	(→6)
suficiente ... ⎭	*enough ...* ⎭	

- '*Than*' followed by a clause is translated by **de lo que** (→7)

Superlatives

These are formed using the following constructions:

el/la/los/las más ... (que)	*the most ... (that)*	(→8)
el/la/los/las menos ... (que)	*the least ... (that)*	(→9)

- After a superlative the preposition **de** is often translated as *in* (→10)

- The absolute superlative (*very, most, extremely* + adjective) is expressed in Spanish by **muy** + adjective, or by adding **-ísimo/a/os/as** to the adjective when it ends in a consonant, or to its stem (adjective minus final vowel) when it ends in a vowel (→11)
  Note that it is sometimes necessary to change the spelling of the adjective when **-ísimo** is added, in order to maintain the same sound (see p 296) (→12)

Continued

1 **una razón más seria**
  a more serious reason
  Es más alto que mi hermano
  He's taller than my brother
2 **una película menos conocida**
  a less well known film
  Luis es menos tímido que tú
  Luis is less shy than you
3 **Pablo tenía tanto miedo como yo**
  Paul was as frightened as I was
4 **No es tan grande como creía**
  It isn't as big as I thought
5 **El examen era tan difícil que nadie aprobó**
  The exam was so difficult that nobody passed
6 **No tengo suficiente dinero para comprarlo**
  I haven't got enough money to buy it
7 **Está más cansada de lo que parece**
  She is more tired than she seems
8 **el caballo más veloz**   **la casa más pequeña**
  the fastest horse   the smallest house
  los días más lluviosos   **las manzanas más maduras**
  the wettest days   the ripest apples
9 **el hombre menos simpático**   **la niña menos habladora**
  the least likeable man   the least talkative girl
  los cuadros menos bonitos   **las camisas menos viejas**
  the least attractive paintings   the least old shirts
10 **la estación más ruidosa de Londres**
   the noisiest station in London
11 **Este libro es muy interesante**   **Tienen un coche rapidísimo**
   This book is very interesting   They have an extremely fast car
   Era facilísimo de hacer
   It was very easy to make
12 **Mi tío era muy rico**   **Se hizo riquísimo**
   My uncle was very rich   He became extremely rich
   un león muy feroz   **un tigre ferocísimo**
   a very ferocious lion   an extremely ferocious tiger

Comparatives and Superlatives (contd)

**Adjectives with irregular comparatives/
superlatives**

ADJECTIVE	COMPARATIVE	SUPERLATIVE
bueno *good*	**mejor** *better*	**el mejor** *the best*
malo *bad*	**peor** *worse*	**el peor** *the worst*
grande *big*	**mayor** *or* **más grande** *bigger; older*	**el mayor** *or* **el más grande** *the biggest; the oldest*
pequeño *small*	**menor** *or* **más pequeño** *smaller; younger; lesser*	**el menor** *or* **el más pequeño** *the smallest; the youngest; the least*

- The irregular comparative and superlative forms of **grande** and
  pequeño are used mainly to express:
  - age, in which case they come after the noun ($\rightarrow$**1**)
  - abstract size and degrees of importance, in which case they
    come before the noun ($\rightarrow$**2**)

  The regular forms are used mainly to express physical size ($\rightarrow$**3**)

- Irregular comparatives and superlatives have one form for both
  masculine and feminine, but always agree in number with the
  noun ($\rightarrow$**1**)

1 **mis hermanos** mayores
my older brothers
la hija menor
the youngest daughter

2 **el** menor **ruido**
the slightest sound
las mayores **dificultades**
the biggest difficulties

3 **Este plato es** más grande **que aquél**
This plate is bigger than that one
Mi casa es más pequeña **que la tuya**
My house is smaller than yours

Demonstrative Adjectives

	MASCULINE	FEMININE	
SING	este	esta	*this*
	ese	esa	
	aquel	aquella	} *that*
PLUR	estos	estas	*these*
	esos	esas	
	aquellos	aquellas	} *those*

- Demonstrative adjectives normally precede the noun and always agree in number and in gender (→1)

- The forms **ese/a/os/as** are used:
  - to indicate distance from the speaker but proximity to the person addressed (→2)
  - to indicate a not too remote distance (→3)

- The forms **aquel/la/los/las** are used to indicate distance, in space or time (→4)

1 **Este bolígrafo no escribe**
This pen is not working
Esa revista es muy mala
That is a very bad magazine
Aquella montaña es muy alta
That mountain (over there) is very high
¿Conoces a esos señores?
Do you know those gentlemen?
Siga Vd hasta aquellos edificios
Carry on until you come to those buildings
¿Ves aquellas personas?
Can you see those people (over there)?

2 **Ese papel en donde escribes ...**
That paper you are writing on ...

3 **No me gustan esos cuadros**
I don't like those pictures

4 **Aquella calle parece muy ancha**
That street (over there) looks very wide
Aquellos años sí que fueron felices
Those were really happy years

214 ADJECTIVES

Interrogative Adjectives

	MASCULINE	FEMININE	
SING	¿qué?	¿qué?	what?, which?
	¿cuánto?	¿cuánta?	how much?; how many?
PLUR	¿qué?	¿qué?	what?, which?
	¿cuántos?	¿cuántas?	how much?; how many?

- Interrogative adjectives, when not invariable, agree in number and gender with the noun (→1)

- The forms shown above are also used in indirect questions (→2)

Exclamatory Adjectives

	MASCULINE	FEMININE	
SING	¡qué!	¡qué!	what (a)
	¡cuánto!	¡cuánta!	what (a lot of)
PLUR	¡qué!	¡qué!	what
	¡cuántos!	¡cuántas!	what (a lot of)

- Exclamatory adjectives, when not invariable, agree in number and gender with the noun (→3)

1 ¿**Qué libro te gustó más?**
  Which book did you like most?
  ¿**Qué clase de hombre es?**
  What type of man is he?
  ¿**Qué instrumentos toca Vd?**
  What instruments do you play?
  ¿**Qué ofertas ha recibido Vd?**
  What offers have you received?
  ¿**Cuánto dinero te queda?**
  How much money have you got left?
  ¿**Cuánta lluvia ha caído?**
  How much rain have we had?
  ¿**Cuántos vestidos quieres comprar?**
  How many dresses do you want to buy?
  ¿**Cuántas personas van a venir?**
  How many people are coming?

2 **No sé a qué hora llegó**
  I don't know at what time she arrived
  Dígame cuántas postales quiere
  Tell me how many postcards you'd like

3 ¡**Qué pena!**
  What a pity!
  ¡**Qué tiempo tan/más malo!**
  What lousy weather!
  ¡**Cuánto tiempo!**
  What a long time!
  ¡**Cuánta pobreza!**
  What poverty!
  ¡**Cuántos autobuses!**
  What a lot of buses!
  ¡**Cuántas mentiras!**
  What a lot of lies!

Possessive Adjectives

Weak forms

WITH SING NOUN		WITH PLUR NOUN		
MASC	FEM	MASC	FEM	
mi	mi	mis	mis	*my*
tu	tu	tus	tus	*your*
su	su	sus	sus	*his; her; its; your (of Vd)*
nuestro	nuestra	nuestros	nuestras	*our*
vuestro	vuestra	vuestros	vuestras	*your*
su	su	sus	sus	*their; your (of Vds)*

- All possessive adjectives agree in number and (when applicable) in gender with the noun, NOT WITH THE OWNER (→1)

- The weak forms always precede the noun (→1)

- Since the form **su(s)** can mean *his, her, your (of Vd, Vds)* or *their*, clarification is often needed. This is done by adding **de él, de ella, de Vds** etc to the noun, and usually (but not always) changing the possessive to a definite article (→2)

Continued

1 **Pilar no ha traído** nuestros libros
Pilar hasn't brought our books
Antonio irá a vuestra casa
Anthony will go to your house
¿Han vendido su coche tus vecinos?
Have your neighbours sold their car?
Mi hermano y tu primo no se llevan bien
My brother and your cousin don't get on

2 su **casa** → la **casa** de él
his house
sus **amigos** → los **amigos** de Vd
your friends
sus **coches** → los **coches** de ellos
their cars
su **abrigo** → el **abrigo** de ella
her coat

Possessive Adjectives (contd)

Strong forms

WITH SING NOUN		WITH PLUR NOUN		
MASC	FEM	MASC	FEM	
mío	**mía**	**míos**	**mías**	*my*
tuyo	**tuya**	**tuyos**	**tuyas**	*your*
suyo	**suya**	**suyos**	**suyas**	*his; her; its; your (of* **Vd***)*
nuestro	**nuestra**	**nuestros**	**nuestras**	*our*
vuestro	**vuestra**	**vuestros**	**vuestras**	*your*
suyo	**suya**	**suyos**	**suyas**	*their; your (of* **Vds***)*

- The strong forms agree in the same way as the weak forms (see p 216)

- The strong forms always follow the noun, and they are used:
  - to translate the English *of mine, of yours*, etc (→**1**)
  - to address people (→**2**)

1 **Es un capricho** suyo
  It's a whim of hers
  un amigo nuestro
  a friend of ours
  una revista tuya
  a magazine of yours

2 **Muy señor** mío (in letters)
  Dear Sir
  hija mía
  my daughter
  ¡Dios mío!
  My God!
  Amor mío
  My love/Darling

Indefinite Adjectives

alguno(a)s	*some*
ambos(as)	*both*
cada	*each; every*
cierto(a)s	*certain; definite*
cualquiera, plur **cualesquiera**	*some; any*
los (las) demás	*the others; the remainder*
mismo(a)s	*same; -self*
mucho(a)s	*many; much*
ningún, ninguna	*any; no*
plur **ningunos, ningunas**	
otro(a)s	*other; another*
poco(a)s	*few; little*
tal(es)	*such (a)*
tanto(a)s	*so much; so many*
todo(a)s	*all; every*
varios(as)	*several; various*

Unless invariable, all indefinite adjectives agree in number and gender with the noun (→**1**)

- **alguno**
  Before a masculine singular noun it drops the final **-o** and adds an accent to show the correct position for stress (→**2**) (see also p 292)

- **ambos**
  Usually it is only used in written Spanish. The spoken language prefers the form **los dos/las dos** (→**3**)

- **cierto** and **mismo**
  They change their meaning according to their position in relation to the noun (see also **Position of Adjectives**, p 224) (→**4**)

- **cualquiera**
  It drops the final **-a** before a masculine *or* feminine noun (→**5**)

Continued

1 **el mismo día**   **las mismas películas**
   the same day   the same films
   mucha/poca gente   **mucho/poco dinero**
   many/few people   much/little money

2 **algún día**   **alguna razón**
   some day   some reason

3 **Me gustan los dos cuadros**
   I like both pictures
   ¿Conoces a las dos enfermeras?
   Do you know both nurses?

4 **cierto tiempo**   *but*   **éxito cierto**
   a certain time   sure success
   el mismo color   *but*   **en la iglesia misma**
   the same colour   in the church itself

5 **cualquier casa**   *but*   **una revista cualquiera**
   any house   any magazine

Indefinite Adjectives (contd)

- **ningún** is only used in negative sentences or phrases (→1)

- **otro**
  It is never preceded by an indefinite article (→2)

- **tal**
  It is never followed by an indefinite article (→3)

- **todo**
  It can be followed by a definite article, a demonstrative or possessive adjective or a place name (→4)

  EXCEPTIONS:
  — when **todo** in the singular means *any, every,* or *each* (→5)
  — in some set expressions (→6)

1 **No es ninguna tonta**
  She's no fool
  ¿No tienes parientes? — No, ninguno
  Haven't you any relatives? — No, none

2 **¿Me das otra manzana?**
  Will you give me another apple?
  Prefiero estos otros zapatos
  I prefer these other shoes

3 **Nunca dije tal cosa**
  I never said such a thing

4 **Estudian durante toda la noche**
  They study all night
  Ha llovido toda esta semana
  It has rained all this week
  Pondré en orden todos mis libros
  I'll sort out all my books
  Lo sabe todo Madrid
  All Madrid knows it

5 **Podrá entrar toda persona que lo desee**
  Any person who wishes to enter may do so
  but
  Vienen todos los días
  They come every day

6 de todos modos   a toda velocidad
   anyway   at full/top speed
   por todas partes ⎫
   por todos lados ⎪
   a/en todas partes ⎬ everywhere
   a/en todos lados ⎭

Position of Adjectives

- Spanish adjectives usually follow the noun (→1, 2)

- Note that when used figuratively or to express a quality already inherent in the noun, adjectives can precede the noun (→3)

- As in English, demonstrative, possessive (weak forms), numerical, interrogative and exclamatory adjectives precede the noun (→4)

- Indefinite adjectives also usually precede the noun (→5)
  But note that **alguno** *some* in negative expressions follows the noun (→6)

- Some adjectives can precede or follow the noun, but their meaning varies according to their position:

BEFORE NOUN		AFTER NOUN	
antiguo	*former*	*old, ancient*	(→7)
diferente	*various*	*different*	(→8)
grande	*great*	*big*	(→9)
medio	*half*	*average*	(→10)
mismo	*same*	*-self, very/precisely*	(→11)
nuevo	*new, another, fresh*	*brand new*	(→12)
pobre	*poor (wretched)*	*poor (not rich)*	(→13)
puro	*sheer, mere*	*pure (clear)*	(→14)
varios	*several*	*various, different*	(→15)
viejo	*old (long known, etc)*	*old (aged)*	(→16)

- Adjectives following the noun are linked by **y** (→17)

1 **la página siguiente**   **la hora exacta**
   the following page   the right time
2 **una corbata azul**   **una palabra española**
   a blue tie   a Spanish word
3 **un dulce sueño**
   a sweet dream
   un terrible desastre (all disasters are terrible)
   a terrible disaster
4 **este sombrero**   **mi padre**   **¿qué hombre?**
   this hat   my father   what man?
5 **cada día**   **otra vez**   **poco dinero**
   every day   another time   little money
6 **sin duda alguna**
   without any doubt
7 **un antiguo colega**   **la historia antigua**
   a former colleague   ancient history
8 **diferentes capítulos**   **personas diferentes**
   various chapters   different people
9 **un gran pintor**   **una casa grande**
   a great painter   a big house
10 **medio melón**   **velocidad media**
   half a melon   average speed
11 **la misma respuesta**   **yo mismo**   **eso mismo**
   the same answer   myself   precisely that
12 **mi nuevo coche**   **unos zapatos nuevos**
   my new car   (some) brand new shoes
13 **esa pobre mujer**   **un país pobre**
   that poor woman   a poor country
14 **la pura verdad**   **aire puro**
   the plain truth   fresh air
15 **varios caminos**   **artículos varios**
   several ways/paths   various items
16 **un viejo amigo**   **esas toallas viejas**
   an old friend   those old towels
17 **una acción cobarde y falsa**
   a cowardly, deceitful act

226 PRONOUNS

Personal Pronouns

PERSON	SINGULAR	PLURAL
	SUBJECT PRONOUNS	
1st	**yo**	**nosotros**
	I	*we* (masc/masc + fem)
		nosotras
		we (all fem)
2nd	**tú**	**vosotros**
	you	*you* (masc/masc + fem)
		vosotras
		you (all fem)
3rd	**él**	**ellos**
	he; it	*they* (masc/masc + fem)
	ella	**ellas**
	she; it	*they* (all fem)
	usted (Vd)	**ustedes (Vds)**
	you	*you*

- Subject pronouns have a limited usage in Spanish. Normally they are only used:
  - for emphasis (→1)
  - for clarity (→2)
  EXCEPTIONS: **Vd** and **Vds** should always be used for politeness, whether they are otherwise needed or not (→3)
- *It* as subject and *they*, referring to things, are never translated into Spanish (→4)
- **tú/usted**
  As a general rule, you should use **tú** (or **vosotros**, if plural) when addressing a friend, a child, a relative, someone you know well, or when invited to do so. In all other cases, use **usted** (or **ustedes**)
- **nosotros/as; vosotros/as; él/ella; ellos/ellas**
  All these forms reflect the number and gender of the noun(s) they replace. **Nosotros, vosotros** and **ellos** also replace a combination of masculine and feminine nouns.

Continued

1 **Ellos sí que llegaron tarde**
They really did arrive late
Tú no tienes por qué venir
There is no reason for you to come
Ella jamás creería eso
She would never believe that

2 **Yo estudio español pero él estudia francés**
I study Spanish but he studies French
Ella era muy deportista pero él prefería jugar a las cartas
She was a sporty type but he preferred to play cards
Vosotros saldréis primero y nosotros os seguiremos
You leave first and we will follow you

3 **Pase Vd por aquí**
Please come this way
¿Habían estado Vds antes en esta ciudad?
Had you been to this town before?

4 **¿Qué es? — Es una sorpresa**
What is it? — It's a surprise
¿Qué son? — Son abrelatas
What are they? — They are tin-openers

Personal Pronouns (contd)

	DIRECT OBJECT PRONOUNS	
PERSON	SINGULAR	PLURAL
1st	**me**	**nos**
	me	*us*
2nd	**te**	**os**
	you	*you*
3rd (masculine)	**lo**	**los**
	him; it; you	*them; you*
	(of Vd)	*(of Vds)*
(feminine)	**la**	**las**
	her; it; you	*them; you*
	(of Vd)	*(of Vds)*

- **lo** sometimes functions as a 'neuter' pronoun, referring to an idea or information contained in a previous statement or question. It is often not translated (→**1**)

Position of direct object pronouns

- In constructions other than the imperative affirmative, infinitive or gerund, the pronoun always comes before the verb (→**2**)
  In the imperative affirmative, infinitive and gerund, the pronoun follows the verb and is attached to it. An accent is needed in certain cases to show the correct position for stress (see also p 292) (→**3**)
- Where an infinitive or gerund depends on a previous verb, the pronoun may be used either after the infinitive or gerund, or before the main verb (→**4**)
  Note how this applies to reflexive verbs (→**4**)
- For further information, see **Order of Object Pronouns**, p 232

Reflexive Pronouns

These are dealt with under reflexive verbs, p 24.

Continued

1 **¿Va a venir María? — No lo sé**
Is Maria coming? — I don't know
Hay que regar las plantas — Yo lo haré
The plants need watering — I'll do it
Habían comido ya pero no nos lo dijeron
They had already eaten, but they didn't tell us
Yo conduzco de prisa pero él lo hace despacio
I drive fast but he drives slowly

2 **Te quiero**
I love you
¿Las ve Vd?
Can you see them?
¿No me oyen Vds?
Can't you hear me?
Tu hija no nos conoce
Your daughter doesn't know us
No los toques
Don't touch them

3 **Ayúdame**   **Acompáñenos**
Help me   Come with us
Quiero decirte algo
I want to tell you something
Estaban persiguiéndonos
They were coming after us

4 **Lo está comiendo** or **Está comiéndolo**
She is eating it
Nos vienen a ver or **Vienen a vernos**
They are coming to see us
No quería levantarse or **No se quería levantar**
He didn't want to get up
Estoy afeitándome or **Me estoy afeitando**
I'm shaving

Personal Pronouns (contd)

INDIRECT OBJECT PRONOUNS

PERSON	*SINGULAR*	*PLURAL*
1st	**me**	**nos**
2nd	**te**	**os**
3rd	**le**	**les**

- The pronouns shown in the above table replace the preposition **a** + noun (→**1**)

Position of indirect object pronouns

- In constructions other than the imperative affirmative, the infinitive or the gerund, the pronoun comes before the verb (→**2**)
  In the imperative affirmative, infinitive and gerund, the pronoun follows the verb and is attached to it. An accent is needed in certain cases to show the correct position for stress (see also p 292) (→**3**)

- Where an infinitive or gerund depends on a previous verb, the pronoun may be used either after the infinitive or gerund, or before the main verb (→**4**)

- For further information, see **Order of Object Pronouns**, p 232.

Reflexive Pronouns

These are dealt with under reflexive verbs, p 24

Continued

1 **Estoy escribiendo** a Teresa → **Le estoy escribiendo**
  I am writing to Teresa   I am writing to her
  Da de comer al gato   → **Dale de comer**
  Give the cat some food   Give it some food

2 **Sofía os ha escrito**   **¿Os ha escrito Sofía?**
  Sophie has written to you   Has Sophie written to you?
  Carlos no nos habla
  Charles doesn't speak to us
  ¿Qué te pedían?
  What were they asking you for?
  No les haga caso Vd
  Don't take any notice of them

3 **Respóndame Vd**   **Díganos Vd la respuesta**
  Answer me   Tell us the answer
  No quería darte la noticia todavía
  I didn't want to tell you the news yet
  Llegaron diciéndome que ...
  They came telling me that ...

4 **Estoy escribiéndole** or **Le estoy escribiendo**
  I am writing to him/her
  Les voy a hablar or **Voy a hablarles**
  I'm going to talk to them

Personal Pronouns (contd)

Order of object pronouns

- When two object pronouns of different persons are combined, the order is: indirect before direct, i.e.

| me
te
nos
os | } before { | lo
la
los
las | (→1) |

Note: When two 3rd person object pronouns are combined, the first (i.e. the indirect object pronoun) becomes **se** (→2)

Points to note on object pronouns

- As **le/les** can refer to either gender, and **se** to either gender, singular or plural, sometimes clarification is needed. This is done by adding **a él** *to him*, **a ella** *to her*, **a Vd** *to you* etc to the phrase, usually after the verb (→3)

- When a noun object precedes the verb, the corresponding object pronoun must be used too (→4)

- Indirect object pronouns are often used instead of possessive adjectives with parts of the body or clothing to indicate 'ownership', and also in certain common constructions involving reflexive verbs (see also **The Indefinite Article**, p 198) (→5)

- **Le** and **les** are often used in Spanish instead of **lo** and **los** when referring to people. Equally **la** is sometimes used instead of **le** when referring to a feminine person or animal, although this usage is considered incorrect by some speakers of Spanish (→6)

Continued

1 **Paloma os lo mandará mañana**
  Paloma is sending it to you tomorrow
  ¿Te los ha enseñado mi hermana?
  Has my sister shown them to you?
  No me lo digas
  Don't tell me (that)
  Todos estaban pidiéndotelo
  They were all asking you for it
  No quiere prestárnosla
  He won't lend it to us

2 **Se lo di ayer**
  I gave it to him/her/them yesterday

3 **Le escriben mucho a ella**
  They write to her often
  Se lo van a mandar pronto a ellos
  They will be sending it to them soon

4 **A tu hermano lo conozco bien**
  I know your brother well
  A María la vemos algunas veces
  We sometimes see María

5 **La chaqueta le estaba ancha**
  His jacket was too loose
  Me duele el tobillo
  My ankle is aching
  Se me ha perdido el bolígrafo
  I have lost my pen

6 **Le/lo encontraron en el cine**
  They met him at the cinema
  Les/los oímos llegar
  We heard them coming
  Le/la escribimos una carta
  We wrote a letter to her

Personal Pronouns (contd)

Pronouns after prepositions

- These are the same as the subject pronouns, except for the forms **mí** *me*, **ti** *you* (sing), and the reflexive **sí** *himself, herself, themselves, yourselves* (→1)

- **Con** *with* combines with **mí**, **ti** and **sí** to form
  conmigo *with me*   (→2)
  contigo *with you*
  consigo *with himself/herself etc*

- The following prepositions always take a subject pronoun:
entre	*between, among* (→3)
hasta } **incluso**	*even, including* (→4)
salvo } **menos**	*except* (→5)
según	*according to* (→6)

- These pronouns are used for emphasis, especially where contrast is involved (→7)

- **Ello** *it, that* is used after a preposition when referring to an idea already mentioned, but never to a concrete noun (→8)

- **A él, de él** NEVER contract (→9)

1 **Pienso en ti**
  I think about you
  Es para ella
  This is for her
  Volveréis sin nosotros
  You'll come back without us
  Hablaba para sí
  He was talking to himself
2 **Venid conmigo**
  Come with me
  Lo trajeron consigo
  They brought it/him with them
3 **entre tú y ella**
  between you and her
4 **Hasta yo puedo hacerlo**
  Even I can do it
5 **todos menos yo**
  everybody except me
6 **según tú**
  according to you
7 **¿A ti no te escriben?**
  Don't they write to you?
  Me lo manda a mí, no a ti
  She is sending it to me, not to you
8 **Nunca pensaba en ello**
  He never thought about it
  Por todo ello me parece que ...
  For all those reasons it seems to me that ...
9 **A él no lo conozco**
  I don't know him

¿Son para mí?
Are they for me?
Iban hacia ellos
They were going towards them
Volaban sobre vosotros
They were flying above you

but **¿Hablaron con vosotros?**
       Did they talk to you?

No he sabido nada de él
I haven't heard from him

Indefinite Pronouns

algo	*something, anything*	(→1)
alguien	*somebody, anybody*	(→2)
alguno/a/os/as	*some, a few*	(→3)
cada uno/a	*each (one)*	(→4)
	everybody	
cualquiera	*anybody; any*	(→5)
los/las demás	*the others*	
	the rest	(→6)
mucho/a/os/as	*many; much*	(→7)
nada	*nothing*	(→8)
nadie	*nobody*	(→9)
ninguno/a	*none, not any*	(→10)
poco/a/os/as	*few; little*	(→11)
tanto/a/os/as	*so much; so many*	(→12)
todo/a/os/as	*all; everything*	(→13)
uno ... (el) otro } **una ... (la) otra** }	*(the) one ... the other*	
unos ... (los) otros } **unas ... (las) otras** }	*some ... (the) others*	(→14)
varios/as	*several*	(→15)

● **algo, alguien, alguno**

They can never be used after a negative. The appropriate negative pronouns are used instead: **nada, nadie, ninguno** (see also negatives, p 272) (→16)

1 **Tengo algo para ti**
I have something for you

¿**Viste algo?**
Did you see anything?

2 **Alguien me lo ha dicho**
Somebody said it to me

¿**Has visto a alguien?**
Have you seen anybody?

3 **Algunos de los niños ya sabían leer**
Some of the children could read already

4 **Le dió una manzana a cada uno** ¡**Cada uno a su casa!**
She gave each of them an apple   Everybody go home!

5 **Cualquiera puede hacerlo**
Anybody can do it

Cualquiera de las explicaciones vale
Any of the explanations is a valid one

6 **Yo me fui, los demás se quedaron**
I went, the others stayed

7 **Muchas de las casas no tenían jardín**
Many of the houses didn't have a garden

8 ¿**Qué tienes en la mano?** — **Nada**
What have you got in your hand? — Nothing

9 ¿**A quién ves?** — **A nadie**
Who can you see? — Nobody

10 ¿**Cuántas tienes?** — **Ninguna**
How many have you got? — None

11 **Había muchos cuadros, pero vi pocos que me gustaran**
There were many pictures, but I saw few I liked

12 ¿**Se oía mucho ruido?** — **No tanto**
Was it very noisy? — Not so very

13 **Lo ha estropeado todo**
He has spoiled everything

Todo va bien
All is going well

14 **Unos cuestan 300 pesetas, los otros 400 pesetas**
Some cost 300 pesetas, the others 400 pesetas

15 **Varios de ellos me gustaron mucho**
I liked several of them very much

16 **Veo a alguien**
I can see somebody

No veo a nadie
I can't see anybody

Tengo algo que hacer
I have something to do

No tengo nada que hacer
I don't have anything to do

Relative Pronouns

PEOPLE		
SINGULAR	*PLURAL*	
que	**que**	*who, that* (subject) (→1)
que	**que**	*who(m), that* (direct object) (→2)
a quien	**a quienes**	
a quien	**a quienes**	*to whom, that* (→3)
de que	**de que**	*of whom, that* (→4)
de quien	**de quienes**	
cuyo/a	**cuyos/as**	*whose* (→5)

THINGS		
SINGULAR AND PLURAL		
que	*which, that* (subject)	(→6)
que	*which, that* (direct object)	(→7)
a que	*to which, that*	(→8)
de que	*of which, that*	(→9)
cuyo	*whose*	(→10)

But note that these forms can also refer to people

- **cuyo** agrees with the noun it accompanies, NOT WITH THE OWNER (→5/10)

- You cannot omit the relative pronoun in Spanish as you can in English (→2/7)

Continued

1 **Mi hermano, que tiene veinte años, es el más joven**
   My brother, who is twenty, is the youngest

2 **Los amigos que más quiero son ...**
   The friends (that) I like best are ...
   María, a quien Daniel admira tanto, es ...
   Maria, whom Daniel admires so much, is ...

3 **Mis abogados, a quienes he escrito hace poco, están ...**
   My lawyers, to whom I wrote recently, are ...

4 **La chica de que te hablé llega mañana**
   The girl (that) I told you about is coming tomorrow
   los niños de quienes se ocupa Vd
   the children (that) you look after

5 **Vendrá la mujer cuyo hijo está enfermo**
   The woman whose son is ill will be coming

6 **Hay una escalera que lleva a la buhardilla**
   There's a staircase which leads to the loft

7 **La casa que hemos comprado tiene ...**
   The house (which) we've bought has ...
   Este es el regalo que me ha mandado mi amiga
   This is the present (that) my friend has sent to me

8 **la tienda a que siempre va**
   the shop (which) she always goes to

9 **las injusticias de que se quejan**
   the injustices (that) they're complaining about

10 **la ventana cuyas cortinas están corridas**
   the window whose curtains are drawn

Relative Pronouns (contd)

el cual, el que

- These are used when the relative is separated from the word it refers to, or when it would otherwise be unclear which word it referred to. The pronouns always agree in number and gender with the noun (→1)
  El cual may also be used when the verb in the relative clause is separated from the relative pronoun (→2)

lo que, lo cual

- The neuter form **lo** is normally used when referring to an idea, statement or abstract noun. In certain expressions, the form **lo cual** may also be used as the subject of the relative clause (→3)

Relative pronouns after prepositions

- **Que** and **quienes** are generally used after the prepositions:

a	*to* (→4)
con	*with* (→5)
de	*from, about, of* (→6)
en	*in, on, into* (→7)

  It should be noted that **en que** can sometimes by translated by:
  - *where*. In this case it can also be replaced by **en donde** or **donde** (→8)
  - *when*. Sometimes here it can be replaced by **cuando** (→9)

- **El que** or **el cual** are used after other prepositions, and they always agree (→10)

Continued

1 **El padre de Elena, el cual tiene mucho dinero, es ...**
Elena's father, who has a lot of money, is ...
(**el cual** *is used here since* que *or* quien *might equally refer to Elena*)
Su hermana, a la cual/la que hacía mucho que no veía, estaba también allí
His sister, whom I hadn't seen for a long time, was also there

2 **Vieron a su tío, el cual, después de levantarse, salió**
They saw their uncle, who, after having got up, went out

3 **No sabe lo que hace**
He doesn't know what he is doing
Lo que dijiste fue una tontería
What you said was foolish
Todo estaba en silencio, lo que (or lo cual) me pareció muy raro
All was silent, which I thought most odd

4 **las tiendas a (las) que íbamos**
the shops we used to go to

5 **la chica con quien (or la que) sale**
the girl he's going out with

6 **el libro de(l) que te hablé**
the book I told you about

7 **el lío en (el) que te has metido**
the trouble you've got yourself into

8 **el sitio en que (en donde/donde) se escondía**
the place where he/she was hiding

9 **el año en que naciste**
the year (when) you were born

10 **el puente debajo del que/cual pasa el río**
the bridge under which the river flows
las obras por las cuales/que es famosa
the plays for which she is famous

Relative Pronouns (contd)

el que, la que; los que, las que

These mean *the one(s) who/which, those who* (→1)
Note that **quien(es)** can replace **el que** *etc* when used in a general
sense (→2)

todos los que, todas las que

These mean *all who, all those/the ones which* (→3)

todo lo que

This translates *all that, everything that* (→4)

el de, la de; los de, las de

These can mean:
   — *the one(s) of, that/those of* (→5)
   — *the one(s) with* (→6)

1 **Esa película es** la que **quiero ver**
That film is the one I want to see
¿Te acuerdas de ese amigo? El que **te presenté ayer**
Do you remember that friend? The one I introduced you to yesterday
Los que quieran entrar tendrán que pagar
Those who want to go in will have to pay

2 **Quien** (*or* el que) **llegue antes ganará el premio**
He who arrives first will win the prize

3 **Todos** los que **salían iban de negro**
All those who were coming out were dressed in black
¿Qué autobuses puedo tomar? — Todos los que **pasen por aquí**
Which buses can I take? — Any (All those) that come this way

4 **Quiero saber** todo lo que **ha pasado**
I want to know all that has happened

5 **Trae la foto de tu novio y** la de **tu hermano**
Bring the photo of your boyfriend and the one of your brother
Viajamos en mi coche y en el de **María**
We travelled in my car and Maria's
Te doy estos libros y también los de **mi hermana**
I'll give you these books and my sister's too

6 **Tu amigo,** el de **las gafas, me lo contó**
Your friend, the one with glasses, told me

Interrogative Pronouns

¿qué?	what?; which?
¿cuál(es)?	which?; what?
¿quién(es)?	who?

qué

It always translates *what* (→1)
Note, however, that **por** + **qué** is normally translated by *why* (→2)

cuál

It normally implies a choice, and translates *which* (→3) EXCEPT when no choice is implied or more specific information is required (→4)
Note that whilst the pronoun **qué** can also work as an adjective, **cuál** only works as a pronoun (→5)

quién

—	**quién(es)** (subject or after preposition)	*who*	(→6)
—	**a quién(es)** (object)	*whom*	(→7)
—	**de quién(es)**	*whose*	(→8)

• All the forms shown above are also used in indirect questions (→9)

1   **¿Qué estan haciendo?**   **¿Qué dices?**
    What are they doing?   What are you saying?
    ¿Para qué lo quieres?
    What do you want it for?

2   **¿Por qué no llegaron Vds antes?**
    Why didn't you arrive earlier?

3   **¿Cuál de estos vestidos te gusta más?**
    Which of these dresses do you like best?
    ¿Cuáles viste?
    Which ones did you see?

4   **¿Cuál es la capital de España?**
    What is the capital of Spain?
    ¿Cuál es tu consejo?
    What is your advice?
    ¿Cuál es su fecha de nacimiento?
    What is your date of birth?

5   **¿Qué libro es más interesante?**
    Which book is more interesting?
    ¿Cuál (de estos libros) es más interesante?
    Which (of these books) is more interesting?

6   **¿Quién ganó la carrera?**
    Who won the race?
    ¿Con quiénes los viste?
    Who did you see them with?

7   **¿A quiénes ayudaste?**   **¿A quién se lo diste?**
    Who(m) did you help?   Who did you give it to?

8   **¿De quién es este libro?**
    Whose is this book?

9   **Le pregunté para qué lo quería**
    I asked him/her what he/she wanted it for
    No me dijeron cuáles preferían
    They didn't tell me which ones they preferred
    No sabía a quién acudir
    I didn't know who to turn to

Possessive Pronouns

These are the same as the strong forms of the possessive adjectives, but they are always accompanied by the definite article.

SINGULAR

MASCULINE	FEMININE	
el mío	**la mía**	*mine*
el tuyo	**la tuya**	*yours* (of **tú**)
el suyo	**la suya**	*his; hers; its; yours* (of **Vd**)
el nuestro	**la nuestra**	*ours*
el vuestro	**la vuestra**	*yours* (of **vosotros**)
el suyo	**la suya**	*theirs; yours* (of **Vds**)

PLURAL

MASCULINE	FEMININE	
los míos	**las mías**	*mine*
los tuyos	**las tuyas**	*yours* (of **tú**)
los suyos	**las suyas**	*his; hers; its; yours* (of **Vd**)
los nuestros	**las nuestras**	*ours*
los vuestros	**las vuestras**	*yours* (of **vosotros**)
los suyos	**las suyas**	*theirs; yours* (of **Vds**)

- The pronoun agrees in number and gender with the noun it replaces, NOT WITH THE OWNER (→1)

- Alternative translations are *my own, your own,* etc (→2)

- After the prepositions **a** and **de** the article **el** is contracted in the normal way (see p 196)

  a + el mío → al mío (→3)
  de + el mío → del mío (→4)

1 **Pregunta a Cristina si este bolígrafo es el suyo**
   Ask Christine if this pen is hers
   ¿Qué equipo ha ganado, el suyo o el nuestro?
   Which team won — theirs or ours?
   Mi perro es más joven que el tuyo
   My dog is younger than yours
   Daniel pensó que esos libros eran los suyos
   Daniel thought those books were his
   Si no tienes discos, te prestaré los míos
   If you don't have any records, I'll lend you mine
   Las habitaciones son menos amplias que las vuestras
   The rooms are smaller than yours

2 **¿Es su familia tan grande como la tuya?**
   Is his/her/their family as big as your own?
   Sus precios son más bajos que los nuestros
   Their prices are lower than our own

3 **¿Por qué prefieres este sombrero al mío?**
   Why do you prefer this hat to mine?
   Su coche se parece al vuestro
   His/her/their car looks like yours

4 **Mi libro está encima del tuyo**
   My book is on top of yours
   Su padre vive cerca del nuestro
   His/her/their father lives near ours

Demonstrative Pronouns

	MASCULINE	FEMININE	NEUTER	
SING	éste	ésta	esto	*this*
	ése	ésa	eso	*that*
	aquél	aquélla	aquello	
PLUR	éstos	éstas		*these*
	ésos	ésas		*those*
	aquéllos	aquéllas		

- The pronoun agrees in number and gender with the noun it replaces (→1)

- The difference in meaning between the forms **ése** and **aquél** is the same as between the corresponding adjectives (see p 212)

- The masculine and feminine forms have an accent, which is the only thing that differentiates them from the corresponding adjectives.

- The neuter forms always refer to an idea or a statement or to an object when we want to identify it, etc, but never to specified nouns (→2)

- An additional meaning of **aquél** is *the former*, and of **éste** *the latter* (→3)

1 **¿Qué** abrigo **te gusta más?** — **Este** de aquí
Which coat do you like best? — This one here
Aquella casa era más grande que ésta
That house was bigger than this one
estos libros y aquéllos
these books and those (over there)
Quiero estas sandalias y ésas
I'd like these sandals and those ones

2 **No puedo creer que** esto **me esté pasando a mí**
I can't believe this is really happening to me
Eso de madrugar es algo que no le gusta
(This business of) getting up early is something she doesn't like
Aquello sí que me gustó
I really did like that
Esto es una bicicleta
This is a bicycle

3 **Hablaban Jaime y Andrés,** éste **a voces y** aquél **casi en un susurro**
James and Andrew were talking, the latter in a loud voice and the former almost in a whisper

Adverbs

Formation

- Most adverbs are formed by adding **-mente** to the feminine form of the adjective. Accents on the adjective are not affected since the suffix **-mente** is stressed independently (→**1**)

  Note, however, that **-mente** is omitted:
  - In the first of two or more of these adverbs when joined by a conjunction (→**2**)
  - In **recientemente** *recently* when immediately preceding a past participle (→**3**). An accent is then needed on the last syllable (see p 292)

- The following adverbs are formed in an irregular way:

bueno	→	**bien**
good		*well*
malo	→	**mal**
bad		*badly*

Adjectives used as adverbs

Certain adjectives are used adverbially. These include:

alto, bajo, barato, caro, claro, derecho, fuerte and **rápido** (→**4**)

It should be noted that other adjectives used as adverbs agree with the subject, and can normally be replaced by the adverb ending in **-mente** or an adverbial phrase (→**5**)

Position of Adverbs

- When the adverb accompanies a verb, it may either immediately follow it or precede it for emphasis (→**6**)

  Note, however, that the adverb can never be placed between **haber** and the past participle in compound tenses (→**7**)

- When the adverb accompanies an adjective or another adverb, it generally precedes the adjective or adverb (→**8**)

Continued

1 *FEM ADJECTIVE*   *ADVERB*
lenta slow   **lenta**mente slowly
franca frank   **franca**mente frankly
feliz happy   **feliz**mente happily
fácil easy   **fácil**mente easily

2 Lo hicieron lenta pero eficazmente
They did it slowly but efficiently

3 El pan estaba recién hecho
The bread had just been baked

4 hablar alto/bajo   **cortar derecho**
to speak loudly/softly   to cut (in a) straight (line)
costar barato/caro   **Habla muy fuerte**
to be cheap/expensive   He talks very loudly
ver claro   **correr rápido**
to see clearly   to run fast

5 Esperaban impacientes (*or* **impacientemente/con impaciencia**)
They were waiting impatiently
Vivieron muy felices (*or* **muy felizmente**)
They lived very happily

6 No conocemos aún al nuevo médico
We still haven't met the new doctor
Aún estoy esperando
I'm still waiting
Han hablado muy bien
They have spoken very well
Siempre le regalaban flores
They always gave her flowers

7 Lo he hecho ya
I've already done it
No ha estado nunca en Italia
She's never been to Italy

8 un sombrero muy bonito   **hablar demasiado alto**
a very nice hat   to talk too loud
mañana temprano   **hoy mismo**
early tomorrow   today

Comparatives and Superlatives

Comparatives

These are formed using the following constructions:

más ... (que)	*more ... (than)*	(→**1**)
menos ... (que)	*less ... (than)*	(→**2**)
tanto como	*as much as*	(→**3**)
tan ... como	*as ... as*	(→**4**)
tan ... que	*so ... that*	(→**5**)
demasiado ... para	*too ... to*	(→**6**)
(lo) bastante ... ⎫		
(lo) suficientemente ... ⎬ **para**	*enough to*	(→**7**)
cada vez más/menos	*more and more/less and less*	(→**8**)

Superlatives

● These are formed by placing **más/menos** *the most/the least* before the adverb (→**9**)

● **lo** is added before a superlative which is qualified (→**10**)

● The absolute superlative (*very, most, extremely* + adverb) is formed by placing **muy** before the adverb. The form **-ísimo** (see also p 292) is also occasionally found (→**11**)

Adverbs with irregular comparatives/superlatives

ADVERB	COMPARATIVE	SUPERLATIVE
bien	**mejor***	**(lo) mejor**
well	*better*	*(the) best*
mal	**peor**	**(lo) peor**
badly	*worse*	*(the) worst*
mucho	**más**	**(lo) más**
a lot	*more*	*(the) most*
poco	**menos**	**(lo) menos**
little	*less*	*(the) least*

***más bien** also exists, meaning *rather* (→**12**)

Continued

1 más **de prisa**   más **abiertamente**
   more quickly   more openly
   Mi hermana canta más **fuerte que yo**
   My sister sings louder than me

2 menos **fácilmente**   menos **a menudo**
   less easily   less often
   Nos vemos menos **frecuentemente que antes**
   We see each other less frequently than before

3 **Daniel no lee tanto como Andrés**
   Daniel doesn't read as much as Andrew

4 **Hágalo** tan **rápido como le sea posible**
   Do it as quickly as you can
   Ganan tan **poco como nosotros**
   They earn as little as we do

5 **Llegaron** tan **pronto que tuvieron que esperarnos**
   They arrived so early that they had to wait for us

6 **Es** demasiado **tarde para ir al cine**
   It's too late to go to the cinema

7 **Eres (lo)** bastante **grande para hacerlo solo**
   You're old enough to do it by yourself

8 **Me gusta el campo cada vez más**
   I like the countryside more and more

9 **María es la que corre** más **rápido**
   Maria is the one who runs fastest
   El que llegó menos **tarde fue Miguel**
   Miguel was the one to arrive the least late

10 **Lo hice lo** más **de prisa que pude**
   I did it as quickly as I could

11 muy **lentamente**   **tempran**ísimo   **much**ísimo
   very slowly   extremely early   very much

12 **Era un hombre** más **bien bajito**
   He was a rather short man
   Estaba más **bien inquieta que impaciente**
   I was restless rather than impatient

254 ADVERBS

Common Adverbs and their usage

bastante	*enough; quite*	(→1)
bien	*well*	(→2)
cómo	*how*	(→3)
cuánto	*how much*	(→4)
demasiado	*too much; too*	(→5)
más	*more*	(→6)
menos	*less*	(→7)
mucho	*a lot; much*	(→8)
poco	*little, not much; not very*	(→9)
siempre	*always*	(→10)
también	*also, too*	(→11)
tan	*as*	(→12)
tanto	*as much*	(→13)
todavía/aún	*still; yet; even*	(→14)
ya	*already*	(→15)

- **bastante, cuánto, demasiado, mucho, poco** and **tanto** are also used as adjectives that agree with the noun they qualify (see indefinite adjectives, p 220 and interrogative adjectives, p 214)

1 **Es bastante tarde**
It's quite late

2 **¡Bien hecho!**
Well done!

3 **¡Cómo me ha gustado!**
How I liked it!

4 **¿Cuánto cuesta este libro?**
How much is this book?

5 **He comido demasiado**   **Es demasiado caro**
I've eaten too much   It's too expensive

6 **Mi hermano trabaja más ahora** **Es más tímida que Sofía**
My brother works more now   She is shyer than Sophie

7 **Se debe beber menos**   **Estoy menos sorprendida que tú**
One must drink less   I'm less surprised than you are

8 **¿Lees mucho?**   **¿Está mucho más lejos?**
Do you read a lot?   Is it much further?

9 **Comen poco**   **María es poco decidida**
They don't eat (very)   Maria is not very daring
much

10 **Siempre dicen lo mismo**
They always say the same (thing)

11 **A mí también me gusta**
I like it too

12 **Ana es tan alta como yo**
Ana is as tall as I am

13 **Nos aburrimos tanto como vosotros**
We got as bored as you did

14 **Todavía/aún tengo dos**   **Todavía/aún no han llegado**
I've still got two   They haven't arrived yet
Mejor aún/todavía
Even better

15 **Ya lo he hecho**
I've done it already

On the following pages you will find some of the most frequent uses of prepositions in Spanish. Particular attention is paid to cases where usage differs markedly from English. It is often difficult to give an English equivalent for Spanish prepositions, since usage *does* vary so much between the two languages. In the list below, the broad meaning of the preposition is given on the left, with examples of usage following. Prepositions are dealt with in alphabetical order, except **a, de, en** and **por** which are shown first.

a

at	**echar algo a algn**	*to throw sth at sb*
	a 50 pesetas el kilo	*(at) 50 pesetas a kilo*
	a 100 km por hora	*at 100 km per hour*
	sentarse a la mesa	*to sit down at the table*
in	**al sol**	*in the sun*
	a la sombra	*in the shade*
onto	**cayeron al suelo**	*they fell onto the floor*
	pegar una foto al álbum	*to stick a photo into the album*
to	**ir al cine**	*to go to the cinema*
	dar algo a algn	*to give sth to sb*
	venir a hacer	*to come to do*
from	**quitarle algo a algn**	*to take sth from sb*
	robarle algo a algn	*to steal sth from sb*
	arrebatarle algo a algn	*to snatch sth from sb*
	comprarle algo a algn	*to buy sth from/for sb**
	esconderle algo a algn	*to hide sth from sb*
means	**a mano**	*by hand*
	a caballo	*on horseback* (but note other forms of transport used with **en** and **por**)
	a pie	*on foot*

**The translation here obviously depends on the context

manner	**a la inglesa**	*in the English manner*
	a pasos lentos	*with slow steps*
	poco a poco	*little by little*
	a ciegas	*blindly*
time, date: *at, on*	**a medianoche**	*at midnight*
	a las dos y cuarto	*at quarter past two*
	a tiempo	*on time*
	a final/fines de mes	*at the end of the month*
	a veces	*at times*
distance	**a 8 km de aquí**	*(at a distance of) 8 kms from here*
	a dos pasos de mi casa	*just a step from my house*
	a lo lejos	*in the distance*
with **el** + infin	**al levantarse**	*on getting up*
	al abrir la puerta	*on opening the door*
after certain adjectives	**dispuesto a todo**	*ready for anything*
	parecido a esto	*similar to this*
	obligado a ello	*obliged to (do) that*
after certain verbs	see p 66	

Personal a

When the direct object of a verb is a person or pet animal, **a** must always be placed immediately before it.

EXAMPLES: **querían mucho a sus hijos**
             they loved their children dearly
             el niño miraba a su perro con asombro
             the boy kept looking at his dog in astonishment
EXCEPTION: **tener**   **tienen dos hijos**
             to have   *they have two children*

Continued

de

from	**venir de Londres**	*to come from London*
	un médico de Valencia	*a doctor from Valencia*
	de la mañana a la noche	*from morning till night*
	de 10 a 15	*from 10 to 15*
belonging to, of	**el sombrero de mi padre**	*my father's hat*
	las lluvias de abril	*April showers*
contents, composition, material	**una caja de cerillas**	*a box of matches*
	una taza de té	*a cup of tea; a tea-cup*
	un vestido de seda	*a silk dress*
destined for	**una silla de cocina**	*a kitchen chair*
	un traje de noche	*an evening dress*
descriptive	**la mujer del sombrero verde**	*the woman with the green hat*
	el vecino de al lado	*the next door neighbour*
manner	**de manera irregular**	*in an irregular way*
	de una puñalada	*by stabbing*
quality	**una mujer de edad**	*an aged lady*
	objetos de valor	*valuable items*
comparative + number	**había más/menos de 100 personas**	*there were more/fewer than 100 people*
after superlatives: *in*	**la ciudad más/menos bonita del mundo**	*the most/least beautiful city in the world*
after certain adjectives	**contento de ver**	*pleased to see*
	fácil/difícil de entender	*easy/difficult to understand*
	capaz de hacer	*capable of doing*
after certain verbs	see p 66	

en

in, at	**en el campo**	*in the country*
	en Londres	*in London*
	en la cama	*in bed*
	con un libro en la mano	*with a book in his hand*
	en voz baja	*in a low voice*
	en la escuela	*in/at school*
into	**entra en la casa**	*go into the house*
	metió la mano en su bolso	*she put her hand into her handbag*
on	**un cuadro en la pared**	*a picture on the wall*
	sentado en una silla	*sitting on a chair*
	en la planta baja	*on the ground floor*
time, dates, months: *at, in*	**en este momento**	*at this moment*
	en 1994	*in 1994*
	en enero	*in January*
transport: *by*	**en coche**	*by car*
	en avión	*by plane*
	en tren	*by train* (but see also **por**)
language	**en español**	*in Spanish*
duration	**lo haré en una semana**	*I'll do it in one week*
after certain adjectives	**es muy buena/mala en geografía**	*she is very good/bad at geography*
	fueron los primeros/ últimos/únicos en + infin	*they were the first/ last/only ones* + infin
after certain verbs	see p 66	

Continued

por

motion: *along, through, around*	**vaya por ese camino** **por el túnel** **pasear por el campo**	*go along that path* *through the tunnel* *to walk around the countryside*

vague
location
	**tiene que estar por
	  aquí**
	**le busqué por todas
	  partes**
		*it's got to be somewhere
		  around here*
		*I looked for him
		  everywhere*

vague time	**por la tarde** **por aquellos días**	*in the afternoon* *in those days*
rate	**90 km por hora** **un cinco por ciento** **ganaron por 3 a 0**	*90 km per hour* *five per cent* *they won by 3 to 0*

agent of
passive:
by
	**descubierto por unos
	  niños**
	odiado por sus enemigos
		*discovered by some
		  children*
		hated by his enemies

by *(means of)*	**por barco** **por tren** **por correo aéreo** **llamar por teléfono**	*by boat* *by train (freight)* *by airmail* *to telephone*
cause, reason: *for, because*	**¿por qué?** **por todo eso** **por lo que he oído**	*why?, for what reason?* *because of all that* *judging by what I've heard*
+ infinitive: *to*	**libros por leer** **cuentas por pagar**	*books to be read* *bills to be paid*
equivalence	**¿me tienes por tonto?**	*do you think I'm stupid?*

+ adjective/
  adverb +
  que:
however
	por buenos que sean
	por mucho que lo quieras
		however good they are
		*however much you
		  want it*

por (contd)

for	¿cuanto me darán por este libro?	how much will they give me for this book?
	te lo cambio por éste	I'll swap you this one for it
	no siento nada por ti	I feel nothing for you
	si no fuera por ti	if it weren't for you
	¡Por Dios!	For God's sake!
for the benefit of	lo hago por ellos	I do it for their benefit
on behalf of	firma por mí	sign on my behalf

por also combines with other prepositions to form double prepositions usually conveying the idea of movement. The commonest of these are:

over	saltó por encima de la mesa	she jumped over the table
under	nadamos por debajo del puente	we swam under the bridge
past	pasaron por delante de Correos	they went past the Post Office
behind	por detrás de la puerta	behind the door
through	la luz entraba por entre las cortinas	light was coming in through the curtains
+ donde	¿por dónde has venido?	which way did you come?

ante

faced with, before	lo hicieron ante mis propios ojos	they did it before my very eyes
	ante eso no se puede hacer nada	one can't do anything when faced with that
preference	la salud ante todo	health above all things

antes de

before (time)	antes de las 5	before 5 o'clock

bajo/debajo de

These are usually equivalent, although **bajo** is used more frequently in a figurative sense and with temperatures.

under	**bajo/debajo de la cama**	*under the bed*
	bajo el dominio romano	*under Roman rule*
below	**un grado bajo cero**	*one degree below zero*

con

with	**vino con su amigo**	*she came with her friend*
after certain adjectives	**enfadado con ellos**	*angry with them*
	magnánimo con sus súbditos	*magnanimous with his subjects*

contra

against	**no tengo nada contra ti**	*I've nothing against you*
	apoyado contra la pared	*leaning against the wall*

delante de

in front of	**iba delante de mí**	*she was walking in front of me*

desde

from	**desde aquí se puede ver**	*you can see it from here*
	llamaban desde España	*they were phoning from Spain*
	desde otro punto de vista	*from a different point of view*
	desde la 1 hasta las 6	*from 1 till 6*
	desde entonces	*from then onwards*
since	**desde que volvieron**	*since they returned*
for	**viven en esa casa desde hace 3 años**	*they've been living in that house for 3 years* (NOTE TENSE)

detrás de

behind   **están detrás de la puerta**   *they are behind the door*

durante

during   **durante la guerra**   *during the war*

for   **anduvieron durante 3 días**   *they walked for 3 days*

entre

between   **entre 8 y 10**   *between 8 and 10*

among   **María y Elena, entre otras**   *Maria and Elena, among others*

reciprocal   **ayudarse entre sí**   *to help each other*

excepto

except (for)   **todos excepto tú**   *everybody except you*

hacia

towards   **van hacia ese edificio**   *they're going towards that building*

around (time)   **hacia las 3**   *at around 3 (o'clock)*
    hacia fines de enero   *around the end of January*

Hacia can also combine with some adverbs to convey a sense of motion in a particular direction:

hacia arriba	*upwards*
hacia abajo	*downwards*
hacia adelante	*forwards*
hacia atrás	*backwards*
hacia adentro	*inwards*
hacia afuera	*outwards*

Continued

hasta

until	**hasta la noche**	*until night*
as far as	**viajaron hasta Sevilla**	*they travelled as far as Seville*
up to	**conté hasta 300 ovejas**	*I counted up to 300 lambs*
	hasta ahora no los había visto	*up to now I hadn't seen them*
even	**hasta un tonto lo entendería**	*even an imbecile would understand that*

para

for	**es para ti**	*it's for you*
	es para mañana	*it's for tomorrow*
	una habitación para dos noches	*a room for two nights*
	para ser un niño, lo hace muy bien	*for a child he is very good at it*
	salen para Cádiz	*they are leaving for Cádiz*
	se conserva muy bien para sus años	*he keeps very well for his age*
+ infin: *(in order) to*	**es demasiado torpe para comprenderlo**	*he's too stupid to understand*
+ sí: *to oneself*	**hablar para sí** **reír para sí**	*to talk to oneself* *to laugh to oneself*
with time	**todavía tengo para 1 hora**	*I'll be another hour (at it) yet*

salvo

except (for)	**todos salvo él**	*all except him*
	salvo cuando llueve	*except when it's raining*
barring	**salvo imprevistos**	*barring the unexpected*
	salvo contraorden	*unless you hear to the contrary*

según

| according to | según su consejo | according to her advice |
| | según lo que me dijiste | according to what you told me |

sin

without	sin agua/dinero	without water/money
	sin mi marido	without my husband
+ infinitive	sin contar a los otros	without counting the others

sobre

on	sobre la cama	on the bed
	sobre el armario	on (top of) the wardrobe
on (to)	póngalo sobre la mesa	put it on the table
about, on	un libro sobre Eva Perón	a book about Eva Perón
above, over	volábamos sobre el mar	we were flying over the sea
	la nube sobre aquella montaña	the cloud above that mountain
approximately:	vendré sobre las 4	I'll come about 4 o'clock
about	Madrid tiene sobre 4 millones de habitantes	Madrid has about 4 million inhabitants

tras

behind	está tras el asiento	it's behind the seat
after	uno tras otro	one after another
	día tras día	day after day
	corríeron tras el ladrón	they ran after the thief

Conjunctions

There are conjunctions which introduce a main clause, such as **y** *and*, **pero** *but*, **si** *if*, **o** *or* etc, and those which introduce subordinate clauses like **porque** *because,* **mientras que** *while,* **después de que** *after* etc. They are used in much the same way as in English, but the following points are of note:

- Some conjunctions in Spanish require a following subjunctive, see pp 60 to 63

- Some conjunctions are 'split' in Spanish like *both ... and, either ... or* in English:

tanto ... como	*both ... and*	(→1)
ni ... ni	*neither ... nor*	(→2)
o (bien) ... o (bien)	*either ... or (else)*	(→3)
sea ... sea	*either ... or,*	(→4)
	whether ... or	

- **y**
  - Before words beginning with **i-** or **hi** + consonant it becomes **e** (→5)

- **o**
  - Before words beginning with **o-** or **ho-** it becomes **u** (→6)
  - Between numerals it becomes **ó** (→7)

- **que**
  - meaning *that* (→8)
  - in comparisons, meaning *than* (→9)
  - followed by the subjunctive, see p 58

- **porque** (Not to be confused with **por qué** *why*)
  - **como** should be used instead at the beginning of a sentence (→10)

- **pero, sino**
  - **pero** normally translates *but* (→11)
  - **sino** is used when there is a direct contrast after a negative (→12)

1 **Estas flores crecen tanto en verano como en invierno**
  These flowers grow in both summer and winter
2 **Ni él ni ella vinieron**
  Neither he nor she came
  No tengo ni dinero ni comida
  I have neither money nor food
3 **Debe de ser o ingenua o tonta**
  She must be either naïve or stupid
  O bien me huyen o bien no me reconocen
  Either they're avoiding me or else they don't recognize me
4 **Sea en verano, sea en invierno, siempre me gusta andar**
  I always like walking, whether in summer or in winter
5 **Diana e Isabel**
  Diana and Isabel
  madre e hija   *but*   **árboles y hierba**
  mother and daughter   trees and grass
6 **diez u once**   **minutos u horas**
  ten or eleven   minutes or hours
7 **37 ó 38**
  37 or 38
8 **Dicen que te han visto**
  They say (that) they've seen you
  ¿Sabías que estábamos allí?
  Did you know that we were there?
9 **Le gustan más que nunca**
  He likes them more than ever
  María es menos guapa que su hermana
  Maria is less attractive than her sister
10 **Como estaba lloviendo no pudimos salir**
   Because/As it was raining we couldn't go out
   (Compare with: **No pudimos salir porque estaba lloviendo**)
11 **Me gustaría ir, pero estoy muy cansada**
   I'd like to go, but I am very tired
12 **No es escocesa sino irlandesa**
   She is not Scottish but Irish

Augmentative, diminutive and pejorative suffixes

These can be used after nouns, adjectives and some adverbs. They are attached to the end of the word after any final vowel has been removed

e.g.	**puerta**	→	**puertita**
	doctor	→	**doctorcito**

Note however that further changes sometimes take place (see p 296)

Augmentatives

These are used mainly to imply largeness, but they can also suggest clumsiness, ugliness or grotesqueness. The commonest augmentatives are:

ón/ona	(→1)
azo/a	(→2)
ote/a	(→3)

Diminutives

These are used mainly to suggest smallness or to express a feeling of affection. Occasionally they can be used to express ridicule or contempt. The commonest diminutives are:

ito/a	(→4)
(e)cito/a	(→5)
(ec)illo/a	(→6)
(z)uelo/a	(→7)

Pejoratives

These are used to convey the idea that something is unpleasant or to express contempt. The commonest suffixes are:

ucho/a	(→8)
acho/a	(→9)
uzo/a	(→10)
uco/a	(→11)
astro/a	(→12)

ORIGINAL WORD	DERIVED FORM
1 **un hombre** a man	**un hombrón** a big man
2 **bueno** good	**buenazo** (person) easily imposed on
un perro a dog	**un perrazo** a really big dog
gripe flu	**un gripazo** a really bad bout of flu
3 **grande** big	**grandote** huge
palabra word	**palabrota** swear word
amigo friend	**amigote** old pal
4 **una casa** a house	**una casita** a cottage
un poco a little	**un poquito** a little bit
un rato a while	**un ratito** a little while
mi hija my daughter	**mi hijita** my dear sweet daughter
despacio slowly	**despacito** nice and slowly
5 **un viejo** an old man	**un viejecito** a little old man
un pueblo a village	**un pueblecito** a small village
una voz a voice	**una vocecita** a sweet little voice
6 **una ventana** a window	**una ventanilla** a small window (car, train etc)
un chico a boy	**un chiquillo** a small boy
una campana a bell	**una campanilla** a small bell
un palo a stick	**un palillo** a toothpick
un médico a doctor	**un mediquillo** a quack (doctor)
7 **los pollos** the chickens	**los polluelos** the little chicks
hoyos hollows	**hoyuelos** dimples
un ladrón a thief	**un ladronzuelo** a petty thief
una mujer a woman	**una mujerzuela** a whore
8 **un animal** an animal	**un animalucho** a wretched animal
un cuarto a room	**un cuartucho** a poky little room
una casa a house	**una casucha** a shack
9 **rico** rich	**ricacho** nouveau riche
10 **gente** people	**gentuza** scum
11 **una ventana** a window	**un ventanuco** a miserable little window
12 **un político** a politician	**un politicastro** a 3rd-rate politician

Word order

Word order in Spanish is much more flexible than in English. You can often find the subject placed after the verb or the object before the verb, either for emphasis or for stylistic reasons (→**1**)

There are some cases, however, where the order is always different from English. Most of these have already been dealt with under the appropriate part of speech, but are summarized here along with other instances not covered elsewhere.

- Object pronouns nearly always come before the verb (→**2**)
  For details, see pp 228 to 231

- Qualifying adjectives nearly always come after the noun (→**3**)
  For details, see p 224

- Following direct speech the subject always follows the verb (→**4**)

For word order in negative sentences, see p 272
For word order in interrogative sentences, see p 276

1 **Ese libro te lo di** yo
  I gave you that book
  No nos vio nadie
  Nobody saw us

2 **Ya los veo**
  I can see them now

  Me lo dieron ayer
  They gave it to me yesterday

3 **una ciudad** española
  a Spanish town

  vino tinto
  red wine

4 — **Pienso que sí — dijo María**
  'I think so,' said Maria
  — **No importa — replicó Daniel**
  'It doesn't matter,' Daniel replied

Negatives

A sentence is made negative by adding **no** between the subject and the verb (and any preceding object pronouns) (→**1**)

There are, however, some points to note:
— in phrases like *not her, not now,* etc the Spanish **no** usually comes after the word it qualifies (→**2**)
— with verbs of saying, hoping, thinking etc *not* is translated by **que no** (→**3**)

Double negatives

no ... nada	*nothing*	*(not ... anything)*
no ... nadie	*nobody*	*(not ... anybody)*
no ... más	*no longer*	*(not ... any more)*
no ... nunca	*never*	*(not ... ever)*
no ... jamás	*never* (stronger)	*(not ... ever)*
no ... más que	*only*	*(not ... more than)*
no ... ningún(o)(a)	*no*	*(not any)*
no ... tampoco	*not ... either*	
no ... ni ... ni	*neither ... nor*	
no ... ni siquiera	*not even*	

Word order

- **No** precedes the verb (and any object pronouns) in both simple and compound tenses, and the second element follows the verb (→**4**)

- Sometimes the above negatives are placed before the verb (with the exception of **más** and **más que**), and **no** is then dropped (→**5**)

- For use of **nada, nadie** and **ninguno** as pronouns, see p 236

Continued

1 AFFIRMATIVE   NEGATIVE
   El coche es suyo   →   **El coche no es suyo**
   The car is his   The car is not his
   Yo me lo pondré   →   **Yo no me lo pondré**
   I will put it on   I will not put it on
2 **¿Quién lo ha hecho? — Ella no**
   Who did it? — Not her
   ¿Quieres un cigarrillo? — Ahora no
   Do you want a cigarette? — Not now
   Dame ese libro, el que está a tu lado no, el otro
   Give me that book, not the one near you, the other one
3 **Opino que no**   **Dijeron que no**
   I think not   They said not
4 **No dicen nada**
   They don't say anything
   No han visto a nadie
   They haven't seen anybody
   No me veréis más
   You won't see me any more
   No te olvidaré nunca/jamás
   I'll never forget you
   No habían recorrido más que 40 kms cuando ...
   They hadn't travelled more than 40 kms when ...
   No se me ha ocurrido ninguna idea
   I haven't had any ideas
   No les estaban esperando ni mi hijo ni mi hija
   Neither my son nor my daughter were waiting for them
   No ha venido ni siquiera Juan
   Even John hasn't come
5 **Nadie ha venido hoy**
   Nobody came today
   Nunca me han gustado
   I've never liked them
   Ni mi hermano ni mi hermana fuman
   Neither my brother nor my sister smokes

Negatives (contd)

Negatives in short replies

- **No**, *no* is the usual negative response to a question (→**1**)
  Note, however, that it is often translated as *not* (→**2**) (see also p 272)

- Nearly all the other negatives listed on p 272 may be used without a verb in a short reply (→**3**)

Combinations of negatives

These are the most common combinations of negative particles:

no ... nunca más	(→**4**)
no ... nunca a nadie	(→**5**)
no ... nunca nada/nada nunca	(→**6**)
no ... nunca más que	(→**7**)
no ... ni ... nunca	(→**8**)

1 ¿Quieres venir con nosotros? — No
Do you want to come with us? — No

2 ¿Vienes o no?
Are you coming or not?

3 ¿Ha venido alguien? — ¡Nadie!
Has anyone come? — Nobody!
¿Has ido al Japón alguna vez? — Nunca
Have you ever been to Japan? — Never

4 No lo haré nunca más
I'll never do it again

5 No se ve nunca a nadie por allí
You never see anybody around there

6 No cambiaron nada nunca
They never changed anything

7 No he hablado nunca más que con su mujer
I've only ever spoken to his wife

8 No me ha escrito ni llamado por teléfono nunca
He/she has never written to me or phoned me

Question forms

Direct

There are two ways of forming direct questions in Spanish:

- by inverting the normal word order so that
  subject + verb → verb + subject (→**1**)

- by maintaining the word order *subject + verb*, but by using a
  rising intonation at the end of the sentence (→**2**)

It should be noted that in compound tenses the auxiliary may
never be separated from the past participle, as happens in English
(→**3**)

Indirect

An indirect question is one that is 'reported', e.g. he asked me
what the time was, tell me *which way to go*. Word order in
indirect questions can adopt one of the two following patterns:

- interrogative word + subject + verb (→**4**)

- interrogative word + verb + subject (→**5**)

¿verdad?, ¿no?

These are used wherever English would use *isn't it?, don't they?,
weren't we?, is it?* etc tagged on to the end of a sentence (→**6**)

sí

Sí is the word for yes in answer to a question put either in the
affirmative or in the negative (→**7**)

1 **¿Vendrá tu madre?**
Will your mother come?
¿Es posible eso?
Is it possible?

¿Lo trajo Vd?
Did you bring it?
¿Cuándo volverán Vds?
When will you come back?

2 **El gato, ¿se bebió toda la leche?**
Did the cat drink up all his milk?
Andrés, ¿va a venir?
Is Andrew coming?

3 **¿Lo ha terminado Vd?**
Have you finished it?

¿Había llegado tu amigo?
Had your friend arrived?

4 **Dime qué autobuses pasan por aquí**
Tell me which buses come this way
No sé cuántas personas vendrán
I don't know how many people will turn up

5 **Me preguntó dónde trabajaba mi hermano**
He asked me where my brother worked
No sabemos a qué hora empieza la película
We don't know what time the film starts

6 **Hace calor, ¿verdad?**
It's warm, isn't it?
No se olvidará Vd, ¿verdad?
You won't forget, will you?
Estaréis cansados, ¿no?
You will be tired, won't you?
Te lo dijo María, ¿no?
Maria told you, didn't she?

7 **¿Lo has hecho? — Sí**
Have you done it? — Yes (I have)
¿No lo has hecho? — Sí
Haven't you done it? — Yes (I have)

Beware of translating word by word. While on occasions this is quite possible, quite often it is not. The need for caution is illustrated by the following:

- English phrasal verbs (i.e. verbs followed by a preposition) e.g. *to run away, to fall down* are often translated by one word in Spanish (→**1**)

- English verbal constructions often contain a preposition where none exists in Spanish, or vice versa (→**2**)

- Two or more prepositions in English may have a single rendering in Spanish (→**3**)

- A word which is singular in English may be plural in Spanish, or vice versa (→**4**)

- Spanish has no equivalent of the possessive construction denoted by *...'s/...s'* (→**5**)

Specific problems
-ing

This is translated in a variety of ways in Spanish:

- *to be ... -ing* can sometimes be translated by a simple tense (see also pp 54 to 56) (→**6**)
  But, when a physical position is denoted, a past participle is used (→**7**)

- in the construction *to see/hear sb ... -ing*, use an infinitive (→**8**)

  -ing can also be translated by:
  — an infinitive (→**9**)
    (see p 46)
  — a perfect infinitive (→**10**)
    (see p 50)
  — a gerund (→**11**)
    (see p 52)
  — a noun (→**12**)

Continued

1 **huir**   **caerse**   **ceder**
to run away   to fall down   to give in
2 **pagar**   **mirar**   **escuchar**
to pay for   to look at   to listen to
encontrarse con   **fijarse en**   **servirse de**
to meet   to notice   to use
3 **extrañarse de**   **harto de**
to be surprised at   fed up with
soñar con   **contar con**
to dream of   to count on
4 **unas vacaciones**   **sus cabellos**
a holiday   his/her hair
la gente   **mi pantalón**
people   my trousers
5 **el coche de mi hermano**   **el cuarto de las niñas**
my brother's car   the children's bedroom
(literally: ... of my brother)   *(literally: ... of the children)*
6 **Se va mañana**   **¿Qué haces?**
He/she is leaving tomorrow   What are you doing?
7 **Está sentado ahí**   **Estaba tendida en el suelo**
He is sitting over there   She was lying on the ground
8 **Les veo venir**   **La he oído cantar**
I can see them coming   I've heard her singing
9 **Me gusta ir al cine**   **¡Deja de hablar!**
I like going to the cinema   Stop talking!
En vez de contestar   **Antes de salir**
Instead of answering   Before leaving
10 **Después de haber abierto la caja, María ...**
After opening the box, Maria ...
11 **Pasamos la tarde fumando y charlando**
We spent the afternoon smoking and chatting
12 **El esquí me mantiene en forma**
Skiing keeps me fit

to be
(See also Verbal Idioms, pp 74 to 76)

- In set expressions, describing physical and emotional conditions, **tener** is used:

tener calor/frío	*to be warm/cold*
tener hambre/sed	*to be hungry/thirsty*
tener miedo	*to be afraid*
tener razón	*to be right*

- Describing the weather, e.g. *what's the weather like?, it's windy/sunny,* use **hacer** (→1)

- For ages, e.g. *he is 6,* use **tener** (see also p 306) (→2)

there is/there are

- Both are translated by **hay** (→3)

can, be able

- Physical ability is expressed by **poder** (→4)

- If the meaning is *to know how to*, use **saber** (→5)

- *Can* + a 'verb of hearing or seeing etc' in English is not translated in Spanish (→6)

to

- Generally translated by **a** (→7)

- In time expressions, e.g. *10 to 6,* use **menos** (→8)

- When the meaning is *in order to*, use **para** (→9)

- Following a verb, as in *to try to do, to like to do*, see pp 46 and 48

- *easy/difficult/impossible* etc *to do* are translated by **fácil/difícil/imposible** etc **de hacer** (→10)

1 **¿Qué tiempo hace?**
What's the weather like?

Hace bueno/malo/viento
It's lovely/miserable/windy

2 **¿Cuántos años tienes?**
How old are you?

Tengo quince (años)
I'm fifteen

3 **Hay un señor en la puerta**
There's a gentleman at the door
Hay cinco libros en la mesa
There are five books on the table

4 **No puedo salir contigo**
I can't go out with you

5 **¿Sabes nadar?**
Can you swim?

6 **No veo nada**
I can't see anything

¿Es que no me oyes?
Can't you hear me?

7 **Dale el libro a Isabel**
Give the book to Isabel

8 **las diez menos cinco**
five to ten

a las siete menos cuarto
at a quarter to seven

9 **Lo hice para ayudaros**
I did it to help you
Se inclinó para atarse el cordón de zapato
He bent down to tie his shoe-lace

10 **Este libro es fácil/difícil de leer**
This book is easy/difficult to read

must

● When *must* expresses an assumption, **deber de** is often used
  (→1)
  Note, however, that this meaning is also often expressed by
  deber directly followed by the infinitive (→2)

● When it expresses obligation, there are three possible
  translations:
  — **tener que**   (→3)
  — **deber**   (→4)
  — **hay que** (impersonal)   (→5)

may

● If *may* expresses possibility, it can be translated by:
  — **poder**
  — **puede (ser) que** + subjunctive   } (→6)

● To express permission, use **poder** (→7)

will

● If *will* expresses willingness or desire rather than the future, the
  present tense of **querer** is used (→8)

would

● If *would* expresses willingness, use the preterite or imperfect of
  querer (→9)

● When a repeated or habitual action in the past is referred to, use
  — the imperfect (→10)
  — the imperfect of **soler** + infinitive (→11)

1 **Ha debido de mentir**
He must have lied
Debe de gustarle
She must like it

2 **Debe estar por aquí cerca**
It must be near here
Debo haberlo dejado en el tren
I must have left it on the train

3 **Tenemos que salir temprano mañana**
We must leave early tomorrow
Tengo que irme
I must go

4 **Debo visitarles**
I must visit them
Debéis escuchar lo que se os dice
You must listen to what is said to you

5 **Hay que entrar por ese lado**
One (We *etc*) must get in that way

6 **Todavía puede cambiar de opinión**
He may still change his mind
Creo que puede llover esta tarde
I think it may rain this afternoon
Puede (ser) que no lo sepa
She may not know

7 **¿Puedo irme?**   **Puede sentarse**
May I go?   You may sit down

8 **¿Quiere Vd esperar un momento, por favor?**
Will you wait a moment, please?
No quiere ayudarme
He won't help me

9 **No quisieron venir**
They wouldn't come

10 **Las miraba hora tras hora**
She would watch them for hours on end

11 **Últimamente solía comer muy poco**
Latterly he would eat very little

Pronunciation of Vowels

Spanish vowels are always clearly pronounced and not relaxed in unstressed syllables as happens in English.

	EXAMPLES	HINTS ON PRONUNCIATION
[a]	casa	Between English *a* as in *hat* and *u* as in *hut*
[e]	pensar	Similar to English *e* in *pet*
[i]	filo	Between English *i* as in *pin* and *ee* as in *been*
[o]	loco	Similar to English *o* in *hot*
[u]	luna	Between English *ew* as in *few* and *u* as in *put*

Pronunciation of Diphthongs

All these diphthongs are shorter than similar English diphthongs.

[ai]	baile, hay	Like *i* in *side*
[au]	causa	Like *ou* in *sound*
[ei]	peine, rey	Like *ey* in *grey*
[eu]	deuda	Like the vowel sounds in English *may you*, but without the sound of the *y*
[oi]	boina, voy	Like *oy* in *boy*

Semi-consonants

[j]	hacia, ya tiene, yeso labio, yo	**i** following a consonant and preceding a vowel, and **y** preceding a vowel are pronounced as *y* in English *yet*
[w]	agua, bueno arduo, ruido	**u** following a consonant and preceding a vowel is pronounced as *w* in English *walk* EXCEPTIONS: **gue, gui** (see p 286)

Pronunciation of Consonants

Some consonants are pronounced almost exactly as in English:
[l, m, n, f, k, and in some cases g]
Others, listed below, are similar to English, but differences should
be noted.

EXAMPLES

[p]	padre	They are not aspirated, unlike
[k]	coco	English *pot*, *cook* and *ten*.
[t]	tan	
[t]	todo, tú	Pronounced with the tip of the
[d]	doy, balde	tongue touching the upper front teeth and not the roof of the mouth as in English.

The following consonants are not heard in English:

EXAMPLES

[ß]	labio	This is pronounced between upper and lower lips, which do not touch, unlike English *b* as in *b*end.
[ɣ]	haga	Similar to English *g* as in *g*ate, but tongue does not touch the soft palate.
[ɲ]	año	Similar to *ni* in on*i*on
[x]	jota	Like the guttural *ch* in lo*ch*
[r]	pera	A single trill with the tip of the tongue against the teeth ridge.
[rr]	rojo, perro	A multiple trill with the tip of the tongue against the teeth ridge.

From spelling to sounds

Note the pronunciation of the following (groups of) letters.

LETTER	PRONOUNCED	
b,v	[b]	These letters have the same value. At the start of a breath group, and after written **m** and **n**, the sound is similar to English *b*oy (→**1**)
	[β]	In all other positions, the sound is unknown in English (see p 285) (→**2**)
c	[k]	Before **a, o, u** or a consonant, like English *k*eep, but not aspirated (→**3**)
	[θ/s]	Before **e, i** like English *th*in, or, in Latin America and parts of Spain, like English *s*ame (→**4**)
ch	[tʃ]	Like English *ch*urch (→**5**)
d	[d]	At the start of the breath group and after **l** or **n**, it is pronounced similar to English *d*eep (see p 285) (→**6**)
	[ð]	Between vowels and after consonants (except **l** or **n**), it is pronounced very like English *th*ough (→**7**)
	[(ð)]	At the end of words, and in the verb ending **-ado**, it is often not pronounced (→**8**)
g	[x]	Before **e, i**, pronounced gutturally, similar to English lo*ch* (→**9**)
	[g]	At the start of the breath group and after **n**, it is pronounced like English *g*et (→**10**)
	[ɣ]	In other positions the sound is unknown in English (→**11**)
gue	[ge/ɣe]	The **u** is silent (→**12**)
gui	[gi/ɣi]	
güe	[gwe/ɣwe]	The **u** is pronounced like English *w*alk (→**13**)
güi	[gwi/ɣwi]	

1 **b**om**b**a   **v**oy   **v**icio
   ['bomba]   [boi]   ['biθjo]

2 hu**b**o   de **v**eras   la**v**ar
   ['ußo]   [de 'ßeras]   [la'ßar]

3 **c**asa   **c**o**c**o   **c**umbre
   ['kasa]   ['koko]   ['kumbre]

4 **c**ero   **c**in**c**o
   ['θero/'sero] ['θiŋko/'siŋko]

5 mu**ch**o   **ch**u**ch**ería
   ['mutʃo]   [tʃutʃe'ria]

6 **d**oy   bal**d**e   bon**d**ad
   [doi]   ['balde]   [bon'dað]

7 mo**d**o   i**d**eal
   ['moðo]   [iðe'al]

8 Ma**d**ri**d**   compra**d**o
   [ma'ðri(ð)]   [kom'pra(ð)o]

9 **g**ente   **g**iro   **g**eneral
   ['xente]   ['xiro]   [xene'ral]

10 **g**anar   pon**g**o
   [ga'nar]   ['poŋgo]

11 a**g**ua   a**g**rícola
   ['aɣwa]   [a'ɣrikola]

12 **gu**ija   **gu**erra   pa**gu**e
   ['gixa]   ['gerra]   ['paɣe]

13 a**gü**ero   ar**gü**ir
   [a'ɣwero]   [ar'ɣwir]

From spelling to sounds (contd)

h	[-]	This is always silent (→**1**)
j	[x]	Like the guttural sound in English lo*ch*, but often aspirated at the end of a word (→**2**)
ll	[ʎ]	Similar to English -*ll*- in mi*lli*on (→**3**)
	[j/ʒ]	In some parts of Spain and in Latin America, like English *y*et or plea*s*ure (→**4**)
-nv-	[mb]	This combination of letters is pronounced as in English *imb*ibe (→**5**)
ñ	[ɲ]	As in English o*ni*on (→**6**)
q	[k]	Always followed by silent letter **u**, and pronounced as in English *k*eep, but not aspirated (→**7**)
s	[s]	Except where mentioned below, like English *s*ing (→**8**)
	[z]	When followed by **b, d, g, l, m, n** like English *z*oo (→**9**)
w	[w]	Like English *v, w* (→**10**)
x	[ks]	Between vowels, often like English e*x*it (→**11**)
	[s]	Before a consonant, and, increasingly, even between vowels, like English *s*end (→**12**)
y	[j]	Like English *y*es (→**13**)
	[ʒ]	In some parts of Latin America, like English lei*s*ure (→**14**)
z	[θ]	Like English *th*in (→**15**)
	[s]	In some parts of Spain and in Latin America, like English *s*end (→**16**)

1 **hombre**   **hoja**   **ahorrar**
['ombre]   ['oxa]   [ao'rrar]

2 **jota**   **tejer**   **reloj**
['xota]   [te'xer]   [re'lo(h)]

3 **calle**   **llamar**
['kaʎe]   [ʎa'mar]

4 **pillar**   **olla**
[pi'jar/pi'ʒar]   ['oja/'oʒa]

5 **enviar**   **sin valor**
[em'bjar]   ['sim ba'lor]

6 **uña**   **bañar**
['uɲa]   [ba'ɲar]

7 **aquel**   **querer**
[a'kel]   [ke'rer]

8 **está**   **serio**
[es'ta]   ['serjo]

9 **desde**   **mismo**   **asno**
['dezðe]   ['mizmo]   ['azno]

10 **wáter**   **Walkman** ®
['bater]   [wak'man]

11 **éxito**   **máximo**
['eksito]   ['maksimo]

12 **extra**   **sexto**
['estra]   ['sesto]

13 **yo**   **yedra**
[jo]   ['jeðra]

14 **yeso**   **yerno**
['ʒeso]   ['ʒerno]

15 **zapato**   **zona**   **luz**
[θa'pato]   ['θona]   [luθ]

16 **zaguán**   **zueco**   **pez**
[sa'ɣwan]   ['sweko]   [pes]

Normal Word Stress

There are simple rules to establish which syllable in a Spanish word is stressed. When an exception to these rules occurs an acute accent (stress-mark) is needed (see p 292). These rules are as follows:

— words ending in a vowel or combination of vowels, or with the consonants **-s** or **-n** are stressed on the next to last syllable. The great majority of Spanish words fall into this category (→**1**)

— words ending in a consonant other than **-s** or **-n** bear the stress on the last syllable (→**2**)

— a minority of words bear the stress on the second to last syllable, and these always need an accent (→**3**)

— some nouns change their stress from singular to plural (→**4**)

Stress in diphthongs

In the case of diphthongs there are rules to establish which of the vowels is stressed (see p 284 for pronunciation). These rules are as follows:

— diphthongs formed by the combination of a 'weak' vowel (**i, u**) and a 'strong' vowel (**a, e** or **o**) bear the stress on the strong vowel (→**5**)
— diphthongs formed by the combination of two 'weak' vowels bear the stress on the second vowel (→**6**)

But note that two 'strong' vowels don't form a diphthong but are pronounced as two separate vowels. In these cases stress follows the normal rules (→**7**)

1 *casa*   *casas*
  house   houses
  co*rre*   **co***rren*
  he runs   they run
  *pala*bra   *pala*bras
  word   words
  cri*sis*   **cri***sis*
  crisis   crises

2 *reloj*
  watch
  *ver***dad**
  truth
  *bati***dor**
  beater

3 *mur*cié*lago*
  bat
  pá*jaro*
  bird

4 *ca***rác**ter   *carac*teres
  character   characters
  ré*gimen*   *regí*menes
  regime   regimes

5 ba*ile*
  dance
  bo*ina*   pe*ine*
  beret   comb
  cau*sa*   re*ina*
  cause   queen

6 *fui*   *viu*do
  I went   widower

7 me *ma***reo**   *ca*er
  I feel dizzy   to fall
  ca*os*   **co***rrea*
  chaos   leash

The acute accent (´)

This is used in writing to show that a word is stressed contrary to the normal rules for stress (see p 290) (→**1**)

The following points should be noted:

- The same syllable is stressed in the plural form of adjectives and nouns as in the singular. To show this, it is necessary to
  - add an accent in the case of unaccented nouns and adjectives ending in **-n** (→**2**)
  - drop the accent from nouns and adjectives ending in **-n** or **-s** which have an accent on the last syllable (→**3**)

- The feminine form of accented nouns or adjectives does not have an accent (→**4**)

- When object pronouns are added to certain verb forms an accent is required to show that the syllable stressed in the verb form does not change. These verb forms are:
  - the gerund (→**5**)
  - the infinitive, when followed by two pronouns (→**6**)
  - imperative forms, except for the 2nd person plural (→**7**)

- The absolute superlative forms of adjectives are always accented (→**8**)

- Accents on adjectives are not affected by the addition of the adverbial suffix **-mente** (→**9**)

1 **auto**b**ús**
  bus
  relámpago
  lightning

2 **orden**   → **órdenes**
  order   orders
  examen   → **exámenes**
  examination   examinations
  joven   → **jóvenes**
  young   young

3 **revolución**   → **revoluciones**
  revolution   revolutions
  autobús   → **autobuses**
  bus   buses
  parlanchín   → **parlanchines**
  chatty   chatty

4 **marqués**   → **marquesa**
  marquis   marchioness
  francés   → **francesa**
  French *(masc)*   French *(fem)*

5 **comprando**   → **compróndo(se)lo**
  buying   buying it (for him/her/them)

6 **vender**   → **vendérselas**
  to sell   to sell them to him/her/them

7 **compra**   → **cómpralo**
  buy   buy it
  hagan   → **hágansclo**
  do   do it for him/her/them

8 **viejo**   → **viejísimo**
  old   ancient
  caro   → **carísimo**
  expensive   very expensive

9 **fácil**   → **fácilmente**
  easy   easily

The acute accent (contd)

It is also used to distinguish between the written forms of words which are pronounced the same but have a different meaning or function. These are as follows:

• Possessive adjectives/personal pronouns (→1)

• Demonstrative adjectives/demonstrative pronouns (→2)

• Interrogative and exclamatory forms of adverbs, pronouns and adjectives (→3)

   Note that the accent is used in indirect as well as direct questions and exclamations (→4)

• The pronoun **él** and the article **el** (→5)

• A small group of words which could otherwise be confused. These are:

de	of, from	**dé**	give (pres subj)	
mas	but	**más**	more	
si	if	**sí**	yes; himself etc	(→6)
solo/a	alone	**sólo**	only	(→7)
te	you	**té**	tea	

The dieresis (¨)

This is used only in the combinations **güi** or **güe** to show that the **u** is pronounced as a semi-consonant (see p 284) (→8)

1 **Han robado mi coche**
They've stolen my car
¿Te gusta tu trabajo?
Do you like your job?

A mí no me vio
He didn't see me
Tú, ¿que opinas?
What do you think?

2 **Me gusta esta casa**
I like this house
¿Ves aquellos edificios?
Can you see those buildings?

Me quedo con ésta
I'll take this one
Aquéllos son más bonitos
Those are prettier

3 **El chico con quien viajé**
The boy I travelled with
Donde quieras
Wherever you want

¿Con quién viajaste?
Who did you travel with?
¿Dónde encontraste eso?
Where did you find that?

4 **¿Cómo se abre?**
How does it open?

No sé cómo se abre
I don't know how it opens

5 **El puerto queda cerca**
The harbour's nearby

Él no quiso hacerlo
HE refused to do it

6 **si nó viene**
if he doesn't come

Sí que lo sabe
Yes he DOES know

7 **Vino solo**
He came by himself

Sólo lo sabe él
Only he knows

8 **¡Qué vergüenza!**
How shocking!
En seguida averigüé dónde estaba
I found out straight away where it was

Regular spelling changes

The consonants **c**, **g** and **z** are modified by the addition of certain verb or plural endings and by some suffixes. Most of the cases where this occurs have already been dealt with under the appropriate part of speech, but are summarized here along with other instances not covered elsewhere.

Verbs

The changes set out below occur so that the consonant of the verb stem is always pronounced the same as in the infinitive. For verbs affected by these changes see the list of verbs on p 81.

INFINITIVE	CHANGE	TENSES AFFECTED	
-car	c + e → -que	Present subj, pret	(→1)
-cer, -cir	c + a, o → -za, -zo	Present, pres subj	(→2)
-gar	g + e, i → -gue	Present subj, pret	(→3)
-guar	gu + e → -güe	Present subj, pret	(→4)
-ger, -gir	g + a, o → -ja, -jo	Present, pres subj	(→5)
-guir	gu + a, o → -ga, -go	Present, pres subj	(→6)
-zar	z + e → -ce	Present subj, pret	(→7)

Noun and adjective plurals

SINGULAR	PLURAL	
vowel + **z**	→ -ces	(→8)

Nouns and adjectives + suffixes

ENDING	SUFFIX	NEW ENDING	
vowel + **z** +	-cito	-cecito	(→9)
-go, -ga +	-ito, -illo	-guito/a, -guillo/a	(→10)
-co, -ca +	-ito, -illo	-quito/a, -quillo/a	(→11)

Adjective absolute superlatives

ENDING	SUPERLATIVE	
-co	-quísimo	(→12)
-go	-guísimo	(→13)
vowel + **z**	-císimo	(→14)

1 **Es inútil que lo busques aquí**
   It's no good looking for it here
   Saqué dos entradas
   I got two tickets
2 **Hace falta que venzas tu miedo**
   You must overcome your fear
3 **No creo que lleguemos antes**
   I don't think we'll be there any sooner
   Ya le pagué
   I've already paid her
4 **Averigüé dónde estaba la casa**
   I found out where the house was
5 **Cojo el autobús, es más barato**
   I take the bus, it's cheaper
6 **¿Sigo?**
   Shall I go on?
7 **No permiten que se cruce la frontera**
   They don't allow people to cross the border
   Nunca simpaticé mucho con él
   I never got on very well with him

8 **voz → voces**
   voice   voices
   veloz → veloces
   quick

   luz → luces
   light   lights
   capaz → capaces
   capable

9 **luz** → **lucecita**
   light   little light
10 **amigo** → **amiguito**
   friend   chum
11 **chico** → **chiquillo**
   boy   little boy
12 **rico** → **riquísimo**
   rich   extremely rich
13 **largo** → **larguísimo**
   long   very, very long
14 **feroz** → **ferocísimo**
   fierce   extremely fierce

A, a	[a]	**J, j**	['xota]	**R, r**	['erre]
B, b	[be]	**K, k**	[ka]	**S, s**	['ese]
C, c	[θe]	**L, l**	['ele]	**T, t**	[te]
Ch, ch	[tʃe]	**Ll, ll**	['eʎe]	**U, u**	[u]
D, d	[de]	**M, m**	['eme]	**V, v**	['uße]
E, e	[e]	**N, n**	['ene]	**W, w**	['uße'doble]
F, f	['efe]	**Ñ, ñ**	['eɲe]	**X, x**	['ekis]
G, g	[xe]	**O, o**	[o]	**Y, y**	[i'ɤrjeɤa]
H, h	['atʃe]	**P, p**	[pe]	**Z, z**	['θeta]
I, i	[i]	**Q, q**	[ku]		

- The letters are feminine and you therefore talk of **una a**, or **la a**

- Capital letters are used as in English except for the following:
  — adjectives of nationality:

  e.g. **una ciudad alemana**   **un autor español**
       a German town   a Spanish author

  — languages:

  e.g. **¿Habla Vd inglés?**   **Hablan español e italiano**
       Do you speak English?   They speak Spanish and
                                        Italian

  — days of the week:

lunes	Monday
martes	Tuesday
miércoles	Wednesday
jueves	Thursday
viernes	Friday
sábado	Saturday
domingo	Sunday

  — months of the year:

enero	January	**julio**	July
febrero	February	**agosto**	August
marzo	March	**se(p)tiembre**	September
abril	April	**octubre**	October
mayo	May	**noviembre**	November
junio	June	**diciembre**	December

Spanish punctuation differs from English in the following ways:

Question marks

There are inverted question marks and exclamation marks at the beginning of a question or exclamation, as well as upright ones at the end

Indications of dialogue

Dashes are used to indicate dialogue, and are equivalent to the English inverted commas:

  — **¿Vendrás conmigo? — le preguntó María**
  'Will you come with me?' Maria asked him
  Note, however, that when no expression of saying, replying etc follows, only one dash is used at the beginning:
  — **Sí.** 'Yes.'

Letter headings

At the beginning of a letter, a colon is used instead of the English comma:
Querida Cristina: Dear Cristina,   **Muy Sr. mío**: Dear Sir,

Punctuation terms in Spanish

.	punto	!	se cierra admiración
,	coma	" "	comillas (used as '…')
;	punto y coma	"	se abren comillas
:	dos puntos	"	se cierran comillas
…	puntos suspensivos	( )	paréntesis
¿ ?	interrogación	(	se abre paréntesis
¿	se abre interrogación	)	se cierra paréntesis
?	se cierra interrogación	—	guión
¡ !	admiración		
¡	se abre admiración	punto y aparte	new paragraph
		punto final	last full stop

Cardinal numbers (*one, two, three etc*)

cero	0	setenta	70
uno (un, una)	1	ochenta	80
dos	2	noventa	90
tres	3	cien (ciento)	100
cuatro	4	ciento uno(una)	101
cinco	5	ciento dos	102
seis	6	ciento diez	110
siete	7	ciento cuarenta y dos	142
ocho	8	doscientos(as)	200
nueve	9	doscientos(as) uno(una)	201
diez	10	doscientos(as) dos	202
once	11	trescientos(as)	300
doce	12	cuatrocientos(as)	400
trece	13	quinientos(as)	500
catorce	14	seiscientos(as)	600
quince	15	setecientos(as)	700
dieciséis	16	ochocientos(as)	800
diecisiete	17	novecientos(as)	900
dieciocho	18	mil	1.000
diecinueve	19	mil uno(una)	1.001
veinte	20	mil dos	1.002
veintiuno	21	mil doscientos veinte	1.220
veintidós	22	dos mil	2.000
treinta	30	cien mil	100.000
treinta y uno	31	doscientos(as) mil	200.000
cuarenta	40	un millón	1.000.000
cincuenta	50	dos millones	2.000.000
sesenta	60	un billón	1.000.000.000.000

Fractions

un medio; medio(a)	$\frac{1}{2}$
un tercio	$\frac{1}{3}$
dos tercios	$\frac{2}{3}$
un cuarto	$\frac{1}{4}$
tres cuartos	$\frac{3}{4}$
un quinto	$\frac{1}{5}$
cinco y tres cuartos	$5\frac{3}{4}$

Others

cero coma cinco	0,5
uno coma tres	1,3
(el, un) diez por ciento	10%
dos más/y dos	2 + 2
dos menos dos	2 − 2
dos por dos	2 × 2
dos dividido por dos	2 ÷ 2

Points to note on cardinals

- **uno** drops the **o** before masculine nouns, and the same applies when in compound numerals:
  un libro *1 book*, **treinta y un niños** *31 children*

- 1, 21, 31 etc and 200, 300, 400 etc have feminine forms:
  cuarenta y una pesetas *41 pesetas*, **quinientas libras** *£500*

- **ciento** is used before numbers smaller than 100, otherwise **cien** is used:
  ciento cuatro *104 but* **cien pesetas** *100 pesetas,* **cien mil** *100,000* (see also p 206)

- **millón** takes **de** before a noun:
  un millón de personas *1,000,000 people*

- **mil** is only found in the plural when meaning *thousands of:*
  miles de solicitantes *thousands of applicants*

- cardinals normally precede ordinals:
  los tres primeros pisos *the first three floors*

- Note that the full stop is used with numbers over one thousand and the comma with decimals i.e. the opposite of English usage.

Continued

Ordinal numbers *(first, second, third etc)*

primero (primer, primera)	1°,1ª	undécimo(a)	11°,11ª
segundo(a)	2°,2ª	duodécimo(a)	12°,12ª
tercero (tercer, tercera)	3°,3ª	decimotercer(o)(a)	13°,13ª
cuarto(a)	4°,4ª	decimocuarto(a)	14°,14ª
quinto(a)	5°,5ª	decimoquinto(a)	15°,15ª
sexto(a)	6º,6ª	decimosexto(a)	16º,16ª
séptimo(a)	7º,7ª	decimoséptimo(a)	17º,17ª
octavo(a)	8º,8ª	decimoctavo(a)	18º,18ª
noveno(a)	9º,9ª	decimonoveno(a)	19º,19ª
décimo(a)	10º,10ª	vigésimo(a)	20º,20ª

Points to note on ordinals

- They agree in gender and in number with the noun, which they normally precede, except with royal titles:

   la primera vez   **Felipe** segundo
   the first time   Philip II

- **primero** and **tercero** drop the **o** before a masculine singular noun:

   el primer premio   **el tercer día**
   the first prize   the third day

- Beyond **décimo** ordinal numbers are rarely used, and they are replaced by the cardinal number placed immediately after the noun:

   el siglo diecisiete   **Alfonso** doce   **en el piso** trece
   the seventeenth century   Alfonso XII   on the 13th floor

   EXCEPTIONS: **vigésimo(a)** 20th (but not with royal
                                 titles or centuries)
                centésimo(a) 100th
                milésimo(a) 1,000th
                millonésimo(a) 1,000,000th

Numbers: Other Uses

- collective numbers:

un par	2, a couple
una decena (de personas)	about 10 (people)
una docena (de niños)	(about) a dozen (children)
una quincena (de hombres)	about fifteen (men)
una veintena* (de coches)	about twenty (cars)
un centenar, una centena (de casas)	about a hundred (houses)
cientos/centenares de personas	hundreds of people
un millar (de soldados)	about a thousand (soldiers)
miles/millares de moscas	thousands of flies

*20, 30, 40, 50 can also be converted in the same way.

- measurements:

viente metros cuadrados	20 square metres
veinte metros cúbicos	20 cubic metres
un puente de cuarenta metros de largo/longitud	a bridge 40 metres long

- distance:

De aquí a Madrid hay 400 km	Madrid is 400 km away
a siete km de aquí	7 km from here

Telephone numbers

Póngame con Madrid, el cuatro, cincuenta y ocho, veintidós, noventa y tres
I would like Madrid 458 22 93

Me da Valencia, el viente, cincuenta y uno, setenta y tres
Could you get me Valencia 20 51 73

Extensión tres, tres, cinco/trescientos treinta y cinco
Extension number 335

NB In Spanish telephone numbers may be read out individually, but more frequently they are broken down into groups of two. They are written in groups of two or three numbers (never four).

The Time

¿Qué hora es?	*What time is it?*	
Es ... *(1 o'clock, midnight, noon)*		} *It's ...*
Son las ... *(other times)*		
Es la una y cuarto	*It's 1.15*	
Son las diez menos cinco	*It's 9.55*	

00.00	**medianoche; las doce (de la noche)** *midnight, twelve o'clock*	
00.10	**las doce y diez (de la noche)**	
00.15	**las doce y cuarto**	
00.30	**las doce y media**	
00.45	**la una menos cuarto**	
01.00	**la una (de la madrugada)** *one a.m., one o'clock in the morning*	
01.10	**la una y diez (de la madrugada)**	
02.45	**las tres menos cuarto**	
07.00	**las siete (de la mañana)**	
07.50	**las ocho menos diez**	
12.00	**mediodía; las doce (de la mañana)** *noon, twelve o'clock*	
13.00	**la una (de la tarde)** *one p.m., one o'clock in the afternoon*	
19.00	**las siete (de la tarde)** *seven p.m., seven o'clock in the evening*	
21.00	**las nueve (de la noche)** *nine p.m., nine o'clock at night*	

NB When referring to a timetable, the 24 hour clock is used:
las dieciséis cuarenta y cinco 16.45
las veintiuna quince 21.15

¿A qué hora vas a venir? — A las siete
What time are you coming? — At seven o'clock
Las oficinas cierran de dos a cuatro
The offices are closed from two until four
Vendré a eso de/hacia las siete y media
I'll come at around 7.30
a las seis y pico
just after 6 o'clock
a las cinco en punto
at 5 o'clock sharp
entre las ocho y las nueve
between 8 and 9 o'clock
Son más de las tres y media
It's after half past three
Hay que estar allí lo más tarde a las diez
You have to be there by ten o'clock at the latest
Tiene para media hora
He'll be half an hour (at it)
Estuvo sin conocimiento durante un cuarto de hora
She was unconscious for a quarter of an hour
Les estoy esperando desde hace una hora/desde las dos
I've been waiting for them for an hour/since two o'clock
Se fueron hace unos minutos
They left a few minutes ago
Lo hice en veinte minutos
I did it in twenty minutes
El tren llega dentro de una hora
The train arrives in an hour('s time)
¿Cuánto (tiempo) dura la película?
How long does the film last?
por la mañana/tarde/noche
in the morning/afternoon or evening/at night

mañana por la mañana	**ayer por la tarde**
tomorrow morning	yesterday afternoon or evening

anoche	**anteayer**	**pasado mañana**
last night	the day before yesterday	the day after tomorrow

Dates

¿Qué día es hoy? ¿A qué día estamos?	What's the date today?
Es (el) ... Estamos a ...	It's the ...
uno/primero de mayo	1st of May
dos de mayo	2nd of May
veintiocho de mayo	28th of May
lunes tres de octubre	Monday the 3rd of October
Vienen el siete de marzo	They're coming on the 7th of March

NB Use cardinal numbers for dates. Only for the first of the month can the ordinal number sometimes be used.

Years

Nací en 1970
I was born in 1970
el veinte de enero de mil novecientos setenta
(on) 20th January 1970

Other expressions

en los años cincuenta	during the fifties
en el siglo veinte	in the twentieth century
en mayo	in May
lunes (quince)	Monday (the 15th)
el quince de marzo	on March the 15th
el/los lunes	on Monday/Mondays
dentro de diez días	in 10 days' time
hace diez días	10 days ago

Age

¿Qué edad tiene? ¿Cuántos años tiene?	How old is he/she?
Tiene 23 (años)	He/She is 23
Tiene unos 40 años	He/She is around 40
A los 21 años	At the age of 21

The following index lists comprehensively both grammatical terms and key words in English and Spanish.

CollinsBilingual   HarperCollins*Publishers*

This is just *one* of the **Collins Pocket** range of bilingual dictionaries and study aids, which cover the following languages:

Dictionaries

	ISBN
Collins Pocket French Dictionary	0-00-433247-4
Collins Pocket French Dictionary (hardback)	0-00-470105-4
Collins Pocket German Dictionary	0-00-433248-2
Collins Pocket German Dictionary (hardback)	0-00-470106-2
Collins Pocket Spanish Dictionary	0-00-433250-4
Collins Pocket Spanish Dictionary (hardback)	0-00-470310-3
Collins Pocket Italian Dictionary	0-00-433249-0
Collins Pocket Italian Dictionary (hardback)	0-00-470309-X
Collins Pocket Portuguese Dictionary	0-00-433306-3
Collins Spurrell Welsh Dictionary	0-00-433549-X
Collins Pocket Greek Dictionary (paperback)	0-00-470241-7
Collins Shubun English-Japanese Dictionary	0-00-433405-1

Study Aids

Collins Pocket French Grammar	0-00-470155-0
Collins Pocket French Verb Tables	0-00-470154-2
Collins Pocket French 10,000 Words	0-00-470158-5
Collins Pocket German Grammar	0-00-470156-9
Collins Pocket German Verb Tables	0-00-470153-4
Collins Pocket German 10,000 Words	0-00-470157-7
(publication June 1994)	
Collins Pocket Spanish Verb Tables and Grammar	0-00-470275-1

COLLINS
for your PC

Collins Electronic Dictionaries
are now available for use with
your personal computer.

For details write to:
Collins Dictionaries: Dept. RDH
PO Box, Glasgow G4 0NB